REMINISCENCES
OF
SYRACUSE
[N E W   Y O R K]

by

Timothy C. Cheney

Compiled by
Parish B. Johnson
from
Personal Recollections of the Author

HERITAGE BOOKS
2013

HERITAGE BOOKS

AN IMPRINT OF HERITAGE BOOKS, INC.

Books, CDs, and more—Worldwide

For our listing of thousands of titles see our website
at
www.HeritageBooks.com

A Facsimile Reprint
Published 2013 by
HERITAGE BOOKS, INC.
Publishing Division
5810 Ruatan Street
Berwyn Heights, Md. 20740

Originally published in the *Syracuse Daily Standard*
Syracuse, New York, 1857

Reprinted from the Annual Volume of the
Onondaga Historical Association, 1914

International Standard Book Numbers
Paperbound: 978-1-58549-833-8
Clothbound: 978-0-7884-6946-6

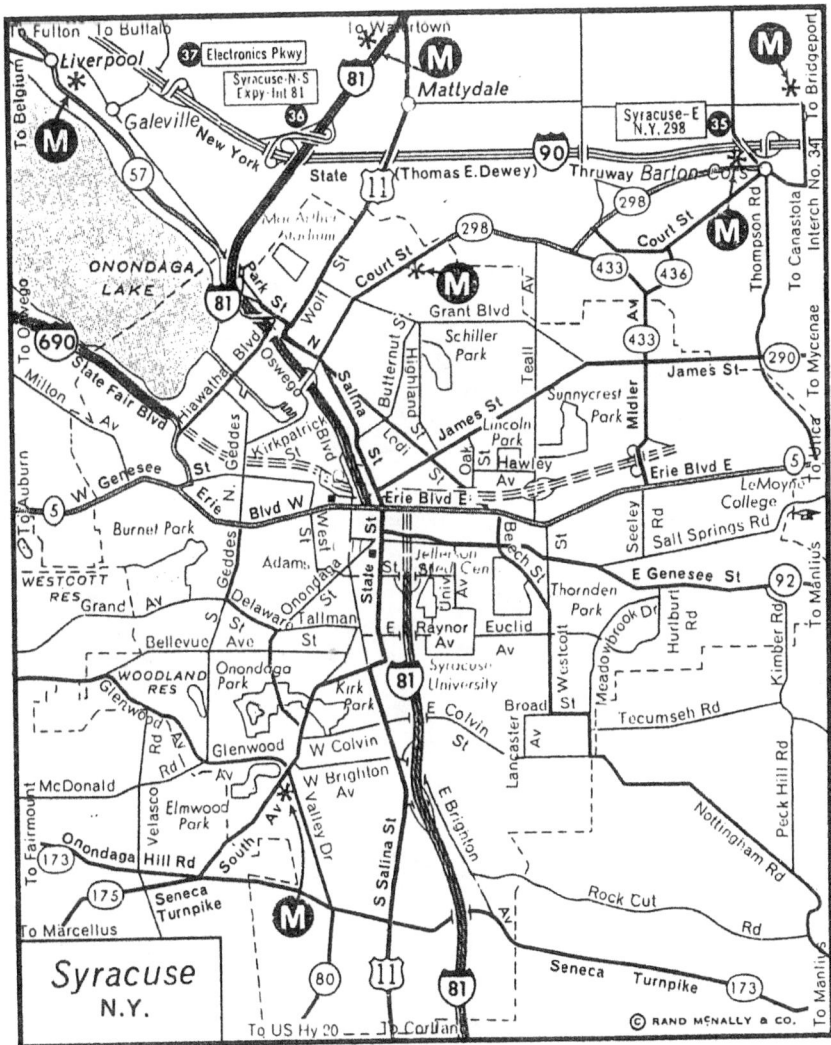
Syracuse N.Y.

PREFACE

In the following pages, the reader is presented with the personal recollections of Mr. T. C. Cheney, one of the oldest and most respected residents of the city of Syracuse.

These recollections consist principally of reminiscences of the early history of the city (or rather the village), its progress in population, wealth and importance, notices of the most important local events that have transpired within its limits, and brief sketches of the early inhabitants of the city and county.

They were prepared at our request for publication in the columns of the Daily and Weekly Standard, and the interest manifested in their perusal, together with the universally expressed desire to obtain then in some better form for preservation, have induced the publishers to issue them in pamphlet form, for the convenience of the public.

Mr. Cheney has been intimately connected with the business and history of the city, and has taken and active part in its development and progress, from the period when it was a small settlement in the swamp, on the banks of Onondaga Creek, until it has proudly taken its place among the cities of the earth, and can boast of as elegant buildings, enterprising inhabitants and liberal institutions as any other place of its size in the Union.

His recollections are given in a plain, discursive and unvarnished style, without any attempt at literary polish, and the typographical execution corresponds with the unpretending style of the work. But they claim the merit of truthfulness, and it is confidently believed that every citizen will be interested in their perusal.

THE PUBLISHERS

SKETCH OF TIMOTHY C. CHENEY'S LIFE
by
MRS. FRANCES M. PALMER

Timothy Collingwood Cheney was born in Rutland, VT, May 7, 1808, being the fourth of the name in a direct line. His great-grandfather was Timothy Cheney, born in Newton, MA, in 1713. It is said that "he was in town office several times", was "ensign of a military company, no empty honor in troublous Indian times and was a man of efficiency". He died in 1772. His son, Timothy was born in 1745, had a large family of large children, and used to joke about his "forty-two feet of boys" which is noticeable from the fact that Mr. Timothy Cheney and his brother, Lucius were each over six feet tall.

The next Timothy, father of Timothy C., was born in Lancaster in 1774, resided in Rutland, VT, until the winter of 1811-12, when he removed to Onondaga County, NY. He left six sons and one daughter, the latter living to the age of ninety-one. Four of these sons lived in Syracuse, two being victims of the gunpowder explosion of Aug. 20, 1841 - H. Nelson and Loren L. Cheney, 35 and 25 years of age respectively. Mr. Nelson Cheney was appointed weighmaster of the U. S. Customs Department at Syracuse, NY, a point rendered important at that time by the Erie Canal, which conveyed passengers and freight in great numbers. He was a politician of influence and a personal friend of Hon. William H. Seward.

Mr. Lucius Cheney, coming with his parents to Onondaga County in 1811, resided in Syracuse until his death in 1880. He was a Selectman of the village three years after its incorporation, and was the father of five sons and one daughter. The fourth of these sons, George Nelson, went into the Battle of Bull Run, July 18, 1861, and "was missing when the battle was over." some of Mr. Lucius Cheney's descendants are still living in this city, among them being George Nelson Cheney and Jerome L. Cheney, his grandsons.

Mr. Timothy Cheney came here with his parents in 1811, and removed to the then village of Syracuse in 1824. He was a contractor and builder, but of the many public edifices that he superintended, only two prominent ones remain - the old Court House now known as the Educational Building, and Renwick Castle, called also after Longstreet and Yates, recently purchased by Syracuse University and used as a Teachers College. Mr. Horatio N. White was the architect of the Court House and Mr. Renwick of New York, the architect of the Castle. The old penitentiary, on the site of the present North High School, was also built by Mr. Cheney, as was one of the Weiting Blocks, fire having devastated the corner at various times. He was chosen Supervisor of the Eighth Ward, and later was made chairman of the Board, an honor seldom conferred on a city member. In 1866 he was Police Commissioner, with E. W. Leavenworth, ex-officio, and Alfred H. Hovey.

In 1832, Mr. Cheney married Ann Belden, daughter of Judge Silas Cook, of Montville, NJ. At Judge Cook's death, in the 85th year of his age, the Morris Palladium said: "As a public individual he was a man whom his fellow citizens delighted to honor. He not only repeatedly filled, with high credit to himself and his constituents, in a high place in the Senate Chamber of his State, but was also for many successive years one of the most distinguished Judges of the courts of his county".

Mrs. Cheney died in Syracuse, Sept. 7, 1855, leaving a family of seven children, three of whom are still living: Mr. Prentice Dana Cheney of Oneida, Mrs. Frances M., wife of A. W. Palmer, and Mrs. Anne P., wife of Salem Hyde, both of this city, where Mr. Cheney died in April 1871, aged sixty-three years.

PARISH B. JOHNSON

COMPILER OF THE REMINISCENCES

The following account of Mr. Johnson was furnished by Miss Mary Potter, a niece of Grove Johnson and cousin of Hiram

Johnson, the present Governor of California", through Mrs. A. W. Palmer.

Parish Barkydt Johnson was born in Washington, NY Nov. 28, 1838, and died in Walla Walla some years ago. He was connected with the Syracuse Daily Standard when it was published by Moses and William Summers, but came to the Pacific coast in 1859 with John F. Kidder, who was sent to Nevada as U. S. Surveyor General. At the outbreak of the Civil War he was made second lieutenant of Company C of the Second California Volunteers, and was promoted to Captain and quarter-master, serving through the war. After peace was declared he settled in Walla Walla, WA - then a territory - and for many years published the Walla Walla Union, a staunch Republican paper. He held various offices and married in that place where he had two children. One died and the other, Dr. Smith S. Johnson, is a practicing physician in Seattle. Mr. Johnson was a strong writer, expressing himself clearly and forcibly, and wielded much influence.

SYRACUSE IN 1824

My father with his family came to this county in the winter of 1811-'12. This county then formed part of the "Military Tract" and was the residence of a large number of Revolutionary soldiers, who had obtained land for their services in our war for freedom. They were generally athletic, hardy, and energetic, and well fitted to settle a new country.

We lived on Onondaga East Hill about two years. My brothers and myself went to school in an old log schoolhouse to our worthy citizen, D. B. Bickford.

A tavern was kept there by Mr. John C. Brown, brother-in-law to Harvey Baldwin, Esq.

Onondaga East Hill was then a place well adapted and frequently used as a rendezvous for regiments of soldiers passing from the Eastern States to the Niagara Frontier.

Fragments of regiments and companies of British prisoners generally camped there for the night by the side of a small stream, while on their way to and from different places of detention or exchange.

I well remember going one fall in a wagon with my father to Salina after a load of salt. We went through Onondaga Hollow by way of Mickles' Furnace, to what was then called the "Corners", now Syracuse. at that time there was no road where the present Tully Plank Road now runs; that part of the county was still in its natural state.

We stopped at a tavern on the present site of the Empire Block, kept by Mr. Bogardus, an old Revolutionary soldier. The house was a small one, and was, I judge, about twenty by thirty feet square and a story and a half high. I do not recollect seeing any other houses, though there may have been two or three small ones.

I well recollect that it was a cedar swamp from the corners of Lodi, and a corduroy road where the Genesee turnpike now runs. The road was covered with an arch of cedars and it looked very much like an arched railroad tunnel, a mile in length. "The Corners" at that time comprised the whole of Syracuse.

At that time nearly all of the first settlers of this county were alive and as a boy, I knew them. I was well acquainted with Gen. Asa Danforth, and used to visit him frequently to listen to his stories about the revolution and partake of the delicious musk melons with he bountifully supplied me.

I was at that time but six years old, and he must have been over seventy-five. I well remember the feelings of sorrow and regret I experienced as I saw him borne to his grave. He was buried on the knoll, next north of the old stone arsenal, and was removed from that place to the family burial ground of Thaddeus M. Wood, and a few years ago his remains were again removed and placed in the cemetery at Onondaga Hollow.

Arthur Patterson and Dr. Needham, of Onondaga Hollow are the only persons now living who acted as pall bearers on that mournful occasion.

General Danforth came to this county in the year 1788, and settled in Onondaga Hollow, with the permission of the Indians.

4

At that time there were a full five hundred Indians belonging to the Onondaga tribe. Many of their old men were engaged in the revolution, They fought for His Majesty, King George the 3rd, against the American forces.

They also fought against General Sullivan soon after the revolution in three small battles in this valley. Two of those battles were fought within the corporate limits of this city.

General Sullivan came up from the Susquehanna with a large force, landed near Elmira, and crossed over the country west of this place, until he reached Onondaga Lake. He passed around the lake until he reached the ground now occupied by the Salt Springs Pump House, which used to be Henry Young's sand bed. At this point he fought a severe battle with the Onondagans and defeated them. The Indians retreated to the foot of the hill where the Water Works Reservoir is now located, and encamped. In the morning General Sullivan sent out his scouts, who discovered and captured a couple Indian spies in a large tree. From these two Indians they obtained information in regard to the camping place of the Onondagas.

The General formed his army in the form of a crescent and advanced over the hill, completely taking the Indians by surprise while busily engaged in cooking breakfast, and shutting out every avenue of escape. At that time the flats near the foot of the hill were covered with water at all seasons of the year.

The Indians, discovering their situation fought like savages while any hope was left, and then wildly plunged into the creek and escaped by swimming. Large numbers of them were killed in the water. General Sullivan rapidly followed up his advantage and completely destroyed the castle and the largest portion of the village.

In the village they found a negro blacksmith engaged in repairing the locks of the Indians' guns. He was immediately seized by the infuriated army and hung and quartered in less than fifteen minutes.

The young chief, Anteauga, was engaged in both these battles, and distinguished himself by his great bravery. He was presented by George Washington with an oblong silver medal which he always wore afterwards, as a token of friendship and fidelity to this government. The medal is probably still in the possession of his relatives on this reservation.

The Onondagas were nearly destroyed by this incursion of General Sullivan into their country. They shortly afterwards came to terms and were thence forward allies of the American Government.

The city was known from 1806 to 1809 as "Bogardus Corners"; from 1809 to 1812 as "Milan"; from 1812 to 1814 as "South Salina"; and from 1814 to 1817 as "Cossitt's Corners"; from 1817 to 1820 as "Corinth"; and from that time it has ever been known as Syracuse, the name given it by John Wilkinson, Esq., he being the first Postmaster.

Mr. Cheney came here to reside in March 1824. He boarded on Church Street, and used to cross "the green" where the old Baptist Church (now the National Theater) stands, on his way to work.

One morning in the spring as he was going to work, the thought came across his mind that he might live to see the time when the "Corners" would become a large and flourishing place, and when that time did arrive, it would be pleasant to look back to the year 1824 and be able to tell how many houses were then erected.

From where he stood every house in the village could be distinctly seen. He counted them and found there were but twenty-three finished houses and six or seven underway.

How few there are, if placed in the same circumstances with Mr. Cheney who would have conceived and carried out such an idea. And yet, that wild dream of the future has come to pass. "The Corners" have grown until now they fill the vast boundaries of Syracuse - the "City of Salt" and "Isms".

At that time it was thought that the "old Red Mill" would be the business center of the future city. What citizen of Syracuse during the past ten years does not remember the old Red Mill? We, the compiler, well remembers its old walls. In our more youthful days it was one of our most favorite places of resort. We remember the feelings of awe and wonder we were wont to experience as we watched the great wooden water-wheel turn, turn, with a uniform motion, as if striving to get rid of the great weight of water, let fall upon its time worn frame from the moss covered flume. We remember curiously watching the tin boxes of the elevator as they would rapidly upward, bearing their burdens of grain or flour; of listening to the ceaseless bur-r-r- of its different run of stone, and the clatter of the hopper as it supplied their greedy mouths. We remember the great bolter and the wooden spout from which it issued a great dusty stream of bran or shorts; the huge box into which was emptied the farmers' bags of grain to be weighed and then let down into the bin below through a square hole in the bottom. And we do not forget the dark frown that would overshadow the fat, jovial face of the miller, as we, boy-fashion, dipped our unresisting hand into the wheat bin, and commenced that great delight of boys making gum.

We remember still later, when the old mill had been abandoned and the great wheel had ceased to turn the complicated machinery. of crowding, burglar-like into one of it back windows and playing hid-and-seek within its deserted walls, of trembling and turning pale as we were startled by the noise made by some ancient rat as it clattered across the floor; as starting noiselessly down the stairs as the declining sun threw a dim and dismal light through its mildewed windows, looking right and left, expecting every instant to behold some ghost or other frightful apparition; until we reached the street, when drawing a deep sigh of relief and casting a sidelong glance at the old mill, we would start on the homeward track; and we remember the old wooden bridge across the creek and race, from which we first witnessed the ceremony of baptism.

Excuse us, kind reader, for indulging in these sweet, sad memories of the past. At times we delight to revel in the shades of other days, and the old Red Mill and the rickety wooden bridge, with many pleasant associations hold a prominent place in our memories.

The old Red Mill was built in 1805, and set in operation the following year by Mr. Walton, of the famous "Walton Tract". It was situated on the east bank of Onondaga Creek, near the present substantial bridge,spanning the creek on West Genesee street. In 1850 the old mill, with its ancient companion, the wooden bridge, was removed to make room for the present artistic superstructure. The motive power was furnished by a mill race, leading from the old mill pond, now Jefferson Park. The mill dam stood where the present Water street bridge has been erected, and the pond extended as far south as Cinder road bridge. The waste water from the mill ran directly into Onondaga Creek. The old mill contained two run of stone, and Henry Young was miller in 1824.

When it became necessary to remove the old mill dam, the Syracuse Company employed Mr. Young to make a pond west of the salt office, to be filled by the waste water from the canal, and to dig a race from the pond to the mill.

While he was engaged in digging the race he removed and old pine stump, standing in from of the dwelling of E. F. Wallace, measuring four feet in diameter. At the foot of the stump among the roots he found the bones of a large Indian, a tomahawk, beads, knives, and a rude earthen pot containing black and red paint. The paint was as fresh and perfect as though mixed the day before. Mr. Young claimed that the bones of this Indian, with the tomahawk, knives and pot of paint had lain there for two hundred years. He had known the spot of ground for forty years and the tree had been cut before he saw the place. The tomahawk found with the Indian is now in the possession of Mr. Cheney. It is a small iron hatchet with a pipe bowl for a head. The handle of this instrument was too much decayed to be preserved. The hatchet must have been brought here by the French Jesuits in 1656, and was obtained from them by this Indian who, to judge from the quantity of trinkets and ornaments buried with him, must have been a very rich man.

A little southwest of the old Red Mill, on the race leading from the dam, Capt. Rufus Parsons built a mill for the purpose of make linseed oil. In 1824 it was in full operation.

Southeast of the oil mill, on the same side of the race, there stood a saw mill. It was built in 1805. In 1824 it was run by Frederick Horner.

That year pine lumber sold at the mill for four dollars per thousand, and hemlock for two dollars and fifty cents. Even at these prices "store pay" had to be taken.

Mr. Hickox built a tannery that year on the present site of Walters' sheep-skin factory. Part of the old building is still standing. Mr. Hickox also built the house on the corner of Mill and Mechanic streets.

In 1824 that portion of our city now occupied by the Syracuse Pump House, was covered with a dense growth of small trees and bushes, Among these trees near the present sand bed stood a gravestone which had been erected many years before to the memory of a poor Indian trader who was murdered on that spot by the Onondagas. The inscription on the gravestone recorded the name of "Benjamin Newkirk, 1787." With Newkirk came a boy by the name of Webster. By reason of some act on their part displeasing to the natives , a council was held, at which it was agreed to kill them. Newkirk they immediately dispatched with a tomahawk. Webster's time had to all appearance come; he was escorted by two Indian to the place of execution. Arrived at the spot he told his conductors that he wanted to drink once more before he died. The request was granted; whereupon he took his cup and drank the health of the Chiefs in a flattering speech. The speech captivated an old man so greatly that he exclaimed "no kill'm". After some parley, he was released and adopted into the tribe. Soon afterward he was married to a squaw. She did not live long. He married another with the understanding that she was to remain his wife as long as she kept sober. He lived with her near twenty years, although he contrived many plots to get her intoxicated, that he might get rid of her and marry a white woman, as the whites became numerous. At the end of this period with the aid of milk punch, he succeeded in this cruel attempts. The morning following her disgrace she arose and without speaking a word, proceeded to gather together her personal effects and left for her friends, no more the wife of Webster. Of a sensitive mind, and possessing a large share of self-respect, grief so preyed upon her that she died in a short time after the separation. One of her sons is now Chief of the Onondagas, and is a man of unblemished character. After his second wife left him, Webster married Catharine Danks, a daughter of one of the early settlers of this county.

Webster was very serviceable in the war of 1812 in commanding the Indians, and acting in the capacity of a spy for General Brown. He was a perfect Indian in manners; he could speak all the dialects of the American and Canadian tribes, and was a very shrewd and sagacious man. He used to make journeys to Canada, and pretending to be intoxicated, lie around the fort at Kingston for the purpose of obtaining information to communicate to the General at Sacketts Harbor. In order to get over the St. Lawrence he would steal a boat, which upon landing on the other side, he would set adrift; and on returning he would repeat the theft. The General and he were in close communion and the nature of their interviews was known only to themselves. When on these Canadian expeditions he would disguise himself with a coloring substance, that gave him the exact appearance of an Indian, and could not be washed off from the skins by any ordinary process. He always pretended that his errand among the red coats was to obtain food or whiskey, and among the officers of recent importation he met with uniform kindness; but the old ones who knew him well, usually sent him away with a kick or a curse.

A little east of Newkirk's grave, myself and other boys used to dig up the remains of Indians, for the purpose of getting possession of beads, kettles, knives, and other implements of warfare, or an ornamental dress that had been buried with them - this being the spot where the slain on both sides in the first battle General Sullivan had with the Onondagas were consigned to their final resting place.

Across the creek of the old Red Mill there were but few houses standing in 1824, and only two or three more built that year.

The house that Hon. George F. Comstock now owns and occupies was occupied that year by John Wall. He boarded the hands employed by Cyprian Hebbard, step-father of George Stevens, Esq. of this city. Mr. Hebbard now resides in Onondaga Valley, and is a man seventy-one years of age. In 1824, Mr. Hebbard was engaged in building the salt works on both sides of Genesee Street, west of the Onondaga Creek.

A small yellow house then stood on the present site od Allen Monroe's new house, and in 1824 was occupied by Sterling Cossitt, formerly landlord of the old Mansion House.

The house now standing on the corner of West and Genesee streets, lately occupied by D. O. Salmon, Esq., was built that year by Henry Young, the miller. His brother, Andrew Young, built the second south of the corner on West street.

Old Mrs. Marble then lived on West Street. Christopher Hyde lived nearly opposite her residence. A carpenter, Patterson lived a little north of Mr. Hyde.

The house Joseph Savage has occupied so many years was built in 1823 and finished in 1824. It was occupied that year by Calvin Mitchell, a contractor. He obtained the contract for the railroad between Schenectady and Albany, one of the first railroads ever built in this State.

These were the only house then standing on the west side of Onondaga creek and north of the canal.

The old house standing on the northeast corner of Genesee and Mill streets, was built several years before by Capt. Rufus Parsons. The house now standing near the northeast corner of Genesee and Mill streets was occupied by Frederick Horner. Mr.

Horner is now nearly 80 years of age and is the only man now living in this city that ever saw George Washington.

About the time of the invention of the grain elevator, inventors experienced great difficulty and expense in obtaining patent rights. Mr, Horner was then engaged in tending mill in New Jersey, and one of the newly invented elevators had been placed in his mill, and as yet had not been patented: though the inventor was using every means in his power to secure the desired protection of his skill. Washington, who was then President, was induced by the invention to diverge from the direct route to the seat of government in New York and witness the performance of the elevator. Thus was Mr. Horner offered the pleasure of exhibiting to the father of his country one of the first grain elevators. This was the only time Mr. Horner ever saw the great Washington, and he remembers him distinctly as he appeared on that occasion.

A little north of Mr. Horner's residence Andrew Young lived in a small wooden house which is now standing.

The house that David Stafford now lives in on West Genesee street was built by his father in 1824. He was a carpenter by trade , and assisted in building the old Baptist church and several other edifices.

A Mr. Cook built the house next west of A. McKinstry's present residence on Church street.

Mr. D. Canfield built the house next east of Public School House No. 4, and that year it was occupied by Rev. Mr. Barlow, the Episcopalian minister.

Samuel Booth was the principal master mason at that time, and owned and lived in a house a little east of Public School House No. 4. He did the mason work on the old Saleratus Factory, and was a prominent, influential mechanic.

An old yellow painted house then stood on the point formed by the junction of Genesee and Church streets, and occupied by Deacon Fellows. The first house next west of the old Baptist church was then standing

Elijah Bicknall built the old Baptist Church that year . Elder Gilbert was Pastor of the church that year, and when the carpenters got ready to raise the building he mounted the timbers and made a long prayer for the blessing and prosperity of their work. Mr. Bicknall also built the small yellow house east of the old church, fronting on Church street.

L. A. Cheney purchased the lot fronting on the corner of Franklin and Mechanic streets that year, for two hundred and fifty dollars. It was then considered one of the most desirable lots in the village, on account of its being so near the center of business. He had his choice and selected that in preference to all others in the village, at the same price. Few persons, if any, then thought that the south side of the canal would ever be anything.

The old wooden house east of the footbridge on Franklin Street was built that year by Matthew L. Davis, and was kept the same year as a tavern by William Hicks. Mr. Davis also built the present residence of William L. Palmer on Genesee street. While Mr. Palmer's family were engaged in cleaning house last spring, they explored a large hole in one of the numerous cupboards, and discovered the remains of a linen pillow case marked "Matthew L. Davis." This pillow case must have lain in that hole upwards of thirty years. It was probably stolen by some mischievous rat and deposited in that place.

A little east of Mr. Hicks tavern, Mr. P. Clarke occupied a small frame house.

The salt fields back of Church street were in full operation that year. The house Mr. Driscoll lived in between Church street and the salt works, was built by Mr. Ryder. He also built two houses on Mill street.

Where Public School House No. 4 now stands there was standing in 1824 an unpainted frame house twenty-five feet square, a story and a half high, with a roof sloping four ways. This building contained one room very high between joists, which was warmed by a large box stove. The room was furnished with old fashioned, inconvenient school house furniture, and in this room William K. Blair, for five and a half days in each week, taught the young ideas of Syracuse how to shoot. The Universalists held regular meetings every Sabbath in this room. The celebrated Orestes A. Brownson, occasionally preached Universalism in this school house to the inhabitants of Syracuse.

The house now occupied by Henry Fellows on West Genesee street was occupied by widow Creed (now Mrs. M. D. Burnet) as a boarding house.

The house on the corner of Franklin and Genesee streets, the present residence of George B. Walters, was built that year by Henry Gifford, Esq.. Mr. Gifford cut some of the sleepers for his house from the ground now occupied by the residence of John Crouse, on the corner of Fayette and Mulberry streets.

Mr. D. Canfield lived in a small house next east of Booth's on Church street. B. Filkins lived next to him on the same side of the street. John Wall built a small house east of Filkin's, for the Syracuse Company.

Miles Seymour built the small house on the southwest corner of Genesee and Franklin streets. He also built and kept a blacksmith shop on the corner of Clinton Alley and Genesee street, the present site of the Dana Block.

Rev. D. Adams lived in a small wooden house on Franklin street between the canal and Genesee street. The house was built in 1824 and occupied by Mr. Adams in 1825.

Mr. Hiram Hyde built the house near the center of the block, between Clinton and Franklin streets.

Henry Newton lived in a small yellow house next west of John Ritchie's new store. The old Eagle Tavern , kept by Frederick Rhyne, then stood on the present site of John Ritchie's store and did a large business.

Joel Cody owned and lived in a small wooden house where the new Baptist church now stands. Attached to his house he had a large, well kept garden, stocked with fruit trees and grapes, running back to Church street. Mr. Cody was at that time Captain of a Packet Boat running between Utica and Rochester, and was noted for his eccentricity and love of fun.

East of Mr. Cody's house two brothers by the name of Woodward built a large frame house, which was kept by them as a hotel for about a year. Afterwards, Mr. Gates, son-in-law of Sterling Cossitt, kept the house, until it was accidentally burned.

The present residence of P. S. Stoddard was occupied in 1824 by Squire Bacon. He kept his Justice Office in the basement.

The present residence of Daniel Dana stood between Woodward's Tavern and a small house standing next to Captain Cody's, occupied by a weak minded man named Cohen. Deacon Dana came here in 1825 and worked in the salt works packing salt.

Monday, July 5th, 1824, marks the date of the first celebration of our National Independence ever held in this city. "The Syracuse Gazette" of July 7th. 1824 published by Mr. Durnford, gives the following account of the celebration:

"At the morn's early dawn the day was ushered in by the thunder of cannon bursting upon the stillness of the hour; and at sunrise a National Salute was fired from Prospect Hill, on the north side of the village. As the spiraling columns of the cannon's smoke disappeared, the star spangled banner of our county was then seen floating majestically in the air, from the top of a towering staff erected on the summit of this hill for the occasion. At about 12 o'clock a procession was formed in front of Mr. Williston's Hotel, under the direction of Col. A. P. Granger, marshal of the day. An escort, consisting of Capt. Rossiter's company of Light Horse, an Artillery Company under the command of Lieut. J. D. Rose and Capt. H. W. Durnford's company of Riflemen, with their music swelling and banners flying, preceded the procession which moved to the new Meeting House (the old Baptist Church.) Here the usual exercises, took place, and an oration was pronounced by J. R. Sutermeister, Esq. which was received by the large assembly with a universal burst of approbation. The procession then formed again and moved through the village to the summit of Prospect Hill, where under a bower a numerous company partook of a cold collation prepared by Mr. Williston (landlord of the Mansion House).

"It was a truly interesting sight to see among our fellow citizens who participated in the festivities of this day. about thirty of them remain of that gallant band of patriots who fought in the revolution. These spared monuments of our country's boast honored the company with their presence throughout the day, giving zest to the festivities rarely to be found in common celebrations of the National Anniversary."

The principal object of attraction on that day was the Rifle company, composed of the young men of the county and commanded by H. W. Durnford, Lieut. James H. Luther and Orderly Zophar H. Adams. They were dressed in red Scotch plaid frocks and pants, trimmed on the bottom and sides with a bright red fringe. They wore leather caps with long red feathers and carried the long Indian rifle, with powder horns and bullet pouches. As they marches through the streets, they presented a gay and imposing appearance.

Prospect Hill was then a full forty feet higher than at present. The trees and bushes were removed from its summit for the purpose of the celebration.

In making a further examination of the files of Mr. Durnford's paper, the Syracuse Gazette, we find the following communication which was published on the 14th of July:

"To Col. Amos P. Granger, and through him to the Committee of Arrangements:

At the request of those soldiers of the revolution present at this day's celebration, the undersigned take the occasion to express their gratitude for the polite and generous attention shown them on this interesting occasion. To us who are now tottering on the down hill of life, whose now feeble limbs were once strong in our country's cause, who went forth to perish or gain that liberty we this day enjoy; the satisfaction of a cheerful welcome, responded by our children and our children's children, cannot fail to reach our hearts and inspire us with respectful gratitude. In you we witness the republican spirit which actuated us in times past, and sustained us in the dreadful conflict, an now holds the world in awe. In the height of your prosperity you were not unmindful of us, a small remnant of the army of the revolution , but conferred on us the honor of leading you to the festive board, under the banners of our hard earned independence. Gentlemen, accept our thanks, and may the God of mercy lengthen your days, strengthened your hands and unite your hearts, in patriotic devotion to the honor and welfare of our beloved country.

s/John Young/Benjamin Darling/Gad Miller/Asa Park/ Henry Bogardus/Peter Bogardus, Committee in Behalf of the '76 men.

Syracuse, July 5, 1824."

These aged veterans fast disappeared, and at the next years celebration only about half the number were present. The second year following they were still fewer in number, and finally all sank into honored graves amid the regrets of every true patriot. In 1824 the thirty veterans who were present walked in the procession on foot, but in the succeeding years time had made so great inroads on their ranks and constitutions that carriages were provided for their accommodation.

A little Irishman named John Dunn, had a blacksmithing and horse shoeing shop next east of Capt. Parsons' house, on the corner of Genesee and Mill streets. He was a jolly whiskey-loving fellow and afforded a great deal of amusement to his customers.

East of David Stafford's house there stood a large painted carriage factory, carried on by a Mr. Martin. Between the factory and Stafford's house there was standing in 1824, a large pine tree.

The old yellow stores, now Taylor & Co.'s Saleratus Factory, were erected in 1824. Samuel Booth had the contract for and performed the mason work of the building. Daniel Elliott of Auburn performed the carpenter work.

Matthew L. Davis occupied the store on the corner of Genesee and Clinton streets as a dry goods store. Heman and Chester Walbridge occupied the store next to him as a dry goods and general assortment. A man from New York kept a bookstore in the same block, in the store next to the canal. The store on Genesee street was occupied by Samuel Hicks as a hat store.

A one and a half story wooden store between the Eagle Tavern and Hicks hat shop was occupied by Matthew L. Davis previous to his going into the corner of the then new block. Before the new stores were completed, the Walbridges occupied the old store formerly standing at the corner of Clinton Alley. B.B. Batchelder occupied a store next to him, an kept a general assortment of all descriptions of goods. A. Root occupied the third store from the corner, as a boot and shoe store. These old buildings were all removed last summer to make room for the new Court House.

Clinton Square, the famous resort for our wood dealers from the country, was then a large green, upon which many a game of base[1] was played by the young men of the village. The packet boats used to land their passengers on the towpath, and they would cross the green to the old Mansion House.

The Mansion House stood on the ground now occupied by the stately Empire Block. It was built in 1805 by Mr. Henry Bogardus, and kept by him as a tavern for many years. Back of the house, Mr. Bogardus erected his barns and out-houses. He also set out a large orchard of apples and other fruit. Some of the old apple trees are still standing and bear a very excellent variety of fruit. Mr. Bogardus had no regular bar in his tavern, and was accustomed to set his liquors and glasses out on a large table.

The Mansion House changed hands several times during its existence. In the spring of 1824 Sterling Cossitt was the landlord.

---

[1] A game similar to "Prisoner's Base.

That spring the house was enlarged and renovated, and O. H. Williston assumed the proprietorship.

The Mansion House was a shabby patched up old concern, requiring additions and alteration ever year, until it looked like a relic of other days. It was the scene of many a hard "Salt Point spree", and had its old walls been gifted with the power of speech, they could have told many a strange tale of hard fought, sternly contested battles between the residents of Salina and Syracuse. The greatest rivalry existed between the town places in 1824 which manifested itself in "free fights" every time the residents crossed the boundary line. That year the Salt Pointers strained every nerve as far as building and business were concerned, to outstrip the rapid growth of Syracuse; but every exertion proved unavailing; Syracuse shot ahead like a race horse and has ever since maintained the ascendency.

In 1845 the old Mansion House and attending buildings were removed to make room for the Empire Block. The Empire Block was commenced in 1845 by John H. Tomlinson and Stephen Cadwell of Syracuse and John Thomas of Albany. The building was finished in 1847, when Mr. Tomlinson became sole owner. Mr. Tomlinson was killed by a railroad accident in Little Falls, in the summer of 1848. He was an active, energetic, enterprising man and carried on more business than ten ordinary men could well accomplish. He was a native of this county, and died deeply regretted by a very extensive acquaintance throughout the State.

In the fall of 1848, the Empire Block was sold under the hammer to John Taylor of Newark, NJ. It was afterward purchased by James L. Voorhees and John D. Norton. In 1850, Col. Vorhees became sole owner, and during the summer of 1856, he made large and important additions and improvements on the original building, until it is now one of the largest, best built and arranged blocks in the city.

Col. Voorhees came to this county in the winter of 1812-13. He settled in Lysander, about 20 miles from the city. The Colonel was then about eighteen years of age. He started in life with an axe, and has hewn himself into a position of great wealth and influence. In his early days the Colonel passed under the familiar nicknames of the "Dutchman" and "the tall pine of Lysander." He has been engaged since his boyhood in the lumber business, in all of its departments, from the office of the "chopper" to the position of the extensive landed proprietor. In the years 1844, '45 and '46 he was engaged in the construction of the extensive Atlantic docks in the port of New York. He is now sixty-two years of age, and appears as hale and hearty as a man of forty, and even now transacts an amount of business that would require the time and energies of three or four common men to accomplish.

In 1824 the people used a peculiar kind of hay scales. A load of hay was drawn under a roof, four chains were lowered and attached to the hubs of the wagon, and by means of pulleys and a windlass the load of hay was hoisted into the air, and the weight determined by a huge pair of steelyards in the loft of the building. Such an inconvenient contrivance for weighing hay stood a little north of the Mansion House.

The house now standing on the southeast corner of Clinton Alley and Church street, now occupied by George B. Parker, Esq., was built in 1824 by Asa Marvin. The house next east of it was built by John Wall for the Syracuse Company.

The present residence of J. D. Dana, Esq. on the corner of Church street and Clinton Alley, was built that year by a Mr. Denslow. The old canal stables on Clinton Alley were in full blast in 1824. They were owned by John A. Green, father of our well known grocery merchant of that name - now part of the New Court House Lot.

In 1824 Gen. A. P. Granger was the proprietor of a store containing a general assortment of all descriptions of wares and merchandise, on the present site of the Star Buildings. Hiram Deming was his clerk. His store was a long two-story building, fronting Salina street. The building stood back from the street a few feet and had a green fence of posts and cross bars between the street and the house, to which his customers fastened their teams when they came to trade. The south end was occupied by the store and the north end of the house and second story, the General occupied as a dwelling house. Between the fence and the house a considerable quantity of shrubbery has been set out, forming a miniature flower garden. The General was one of the principal men of the village, and on the occasion of LaFayette's passage through Syracuse (June 8th, 1825) during his last visit to this country, he was made the orator of the day.

The General performed the duties of the office to the entire satisfaction of every person present on that occasion, by making an excellent and appropriate speech to the assembled citizens from the deck of a canal boat, in honor of the distinguished visitor.

At the time of LaFayette's visit to this place, there lived at Onondaga Hollow a large athletic man named Moore, familiarly known under the appellation of "Donakeedee." This man was engaged in the revolution and served as a private in LaFayette's regiment. While in the army he had been nicknamed on account of his extremely large head, "Cabbage Head." LaFayette came from the west by the way of Marcellus, Onondaga Hill and Onondaga Hollow. While passing through the Hollow, Moore was brought before him and he was asked who it was. LaFayette regarded the man for a moment, and then exclaimed, "Why it's Cabbage Head." This story will serve to show the remarkable memory of the great LaFayette. He had not seen "Cabbage Head" for forty-two years, and his memory of the man was perfect.

A few moments after LaFayette had made his final bow to the assembled citizens, and retired to the cabin of the boat in which he was traveling, a large scow boat loaded with men, women, and children arrived from Geddes to see the great and illustrious companion of Washington. LaFayette being informed of their arrival, again ascended the deck, amid prolonged cheers of the multitude, said a few words to his Geddes visitants , and bowing proceed on his way to Utica.

LaFayette was a man of medium height, well proportioned, and stood very erect for a man of his age, large head, full features, a rough, swarthy skin, and beard cut smooth. He wore a light brown wig, rather inclined to red, and was dressed in a straight bodied black coat, black silk vest, Nankeen pants, and calf skin shoes. He was very polite and pleasing in his address, in fact, a most perfect and polished gentleman in every respect.

LaFayette's son, George Washington LaFayette, accompanied him on his last visit to this country. He was a larger man than his father. The top of his head was bald, what little hair he possessed being brown. He was a very good looking man, free and easy in his manners, and dressed in black.

In 1824, Salina street bridge consisted of one single stone arch, barely high enough to admit the passage of the small boats they used in those days. A stone wall was raised about three feet above the level of the roadway on each side of the bridge, and was covered with flag coping full three feet broad. This wall formed a favorite lounging place for the lazy people of Syracuse. They could lie on the coping and watch the boats as they passed up and down the canal, and at the same time witness all that transpired in the village. Occasionally one of these loafers would go to sleep and roll off into the canal, thus furnishing food for the gossiping tongues of the villagers for many a day and week.

In 1824 Stephen W. Cadwell and Paschal Thurber bought out a man by the name of Cummings, who kept a lot of pet bears, wolves, monkeys and other wild animals on the ground now occupied by Cadwell and the Doran brothers, on James street. This Cummings was a miserable old fellow, and everybody was glad to get rid of him.

Between Cadwell and Granger's corner there were three or four old rookeries standing, occupied by different persons, who derived the principal part of their trade from the canal boatmen.

East of Cadwell's a man named Brockway occupied a little shop as a meat market. Next to the meat market there stood a large frame building painted red, a miserable old shell at best. East of this red house on the corner now occupied as a grocery by B. C. Lathrop, a store house was kept by E. L. Clark in a large wooden building, since burned.

In 1824 that portion of James street styled "Robbers Row," had been surveyed and laid out as a street, but had not been worked. The trees and brush had been cleared off, and the passage of teams had made considerable of a trail. Stores and houses on the south side of the street had their front entrances opening on the towpath. The gable ends and back yards of the houses were on James street.

James street proper was at that time only an Indian trail leading over the hills to what was then Foot Settlement, now the first gate. The eye of the lonely wayfarer on that trail was not gladdened by the sight of the lordly and palatial residences of the upper ten, that now give a grand an aristocratic appearance to this beautiful tract.

The only object on this trail that then served as a resting place to eyes (if there ever were such, wearied with continuous watching of swaying trees and falling leaves in the dense forest, where God speaks to man through the rustling leaves, the sighing wind, and the joyous appearance of all nature as with a human voice) was the dwelling house of Major Burnet, erected that year by Rodney Sargents of Auburn. This house stood on a slight eminence now occupied by the new residence of Major Burnet. The house fronted the south, and had a path or rather an impromptu road leading directly to the towing path on the Erie canal. The house then stood far out of town, and the only avenue of approach for teams was by the tow path and the private road. Persons on foot could reach the house by taking the trail and beating through the underbrush.

The old Collector's office stood between the bridges spanning the junction of the Erie and Oswego canals.

A foundation of hewn timber was laid upon "Goose Island", on the north side of the towing path, and upon this was erected a small frame house, which was designated as the Canal Collector's office. Dr. Colvin was the Collector in 1824, and employed Ben Lathrop and B.F. Colvin as clerks in his office. The Doctor resided in a small frame house on Salina street, a little north of Waggoner's Corners.

The amount of produce cleared during the season of 1824 from this office was 12,065 barrels of flour, 2862 barrels of provisions, 2565 barrels ashes, 76,631 barrels salt and 64,240 bushels of wheat. The amount of toll received at the office during the season of 1824 was $18,491.58.

The old weighlock was completed that year. It was built upon an entirely different plan from the one now followed; the weight of the boat being determined by measuring the quantity of water it displaced.

Deacon Spencer then owned and occupied the old boat yard (now John Durston's), near the Oswego Canal. The boat yard was then considered out of town, the easiest avenue of approach being by the tow path.

Deacon Spencer lived in a small frame house adjoining, and west of the present "Greyhound Inn", on the corner of James and Warren streets. Between Deacon Spencer's residence and Waggoner's corner there were two small edifices. The first one was occupied and used as a blacksmith shop. The other was the residence of Widow Cushing, who obtained a scanty subsistence by retailing milk to those needing this product of her only cow.

A little mercurial Frenchman, named Lewis, a brother-in-law of Sterling Cossitt, resided in the first house north of Dr. Colvin's on Salina Street

James Sackett commenced building in 1824, a little north of Dr. Colvin and the Frenchman. He was a very eccentric man, and at times was feared and disliked by all his neighbors, because he would persist in indulging in the most eccentric habits.   Dr.

Colvin's, the Frenchman's, and Mr. Sacketts' were the only houses on the block opposite the Empire in 1824.

A small frame house stood on the ground now occupied by the Noxon Block. It was then occupied as a dwelling by Isaac Stanton. Amos Stanton, the father of Isaac and Rufus Stanton came here to reside in 1805. He engaged in the manufacturing of salt, during the winter. That article then sold for $3.00 a barrel, and in 1824 is was sold for a dollar and a half per barrel. Mr. Stanton then, in 1805, owned one square acre of ground, including the land now occupied by the old "Ogle Tavern", near the Oswego canal bridge on Salina street. Mr. Stanton had this acre of land cleared and converted into a wheat field. When the Oswego Canal was built they cut diagonally through Mr. Stanton's acre.

The Ogle Tavern was occupied as a private dwelling house in 1824.

Mr. Bogardus, of the Mansion House, built a small frame house near the present site of Corinthian Hall, which he occupied while building the Mansion House. Paschal Thurber lived in it in 1824. The house stood on the bank of a small natural creek, since arched and formed into a sluice way for passage of the surplus water of the new weigh lock.

On the north side of the Oswego Canal the house lately known as "Church's Grocer", then belonged to the widow of Peter Wales, and was occupied by her as a dwelling house. The land north and east of Widow Wales' house was covered by a young growth of trees and underbrush, the only clearing being a patch of ground near the old Centre House, upon which one Harry Blake had built himself a dwelling and commenced to farm it.

There were no other dwellings between Syracuse and Salina. It was then two miles between the two places, and Salina street a mere wagon track cut though the timber and known as Cooper street. The name was derived from the circumstances that several coopers put up shanties and used all the available timber for the purpose of making barrels, about the year 1806.

A little cluster of cheaply built, whitewashed houses , known as White Hall stood on the first block north of the new Catholic church.

I think there were three or four salt blocks standing near the canal. They were built in the old fashioned style with the side towards the canal, a chimney in the middle and a fire built at both ends of the block. I think there were two or three little houses near the blocks occupied by the salt boilers.

With the exception of these few buildings and a little patch of cleared land, formerly part of Stanton's farm, all that portion of the city lying north of the Erie and east of the Oswego canals, was covered with a heavy growth of timber and underbrush, with numerous paths leading to various spots where wood had been cut for the purpose of making salt.

The first lock formerly stood but a few yards east of Mulberry street bridge. "Vinegar Hill" then, as now, consisted of several shanties and old rookeries, erected there to catch the trade of the passing boatmen. In 1840 Captain Joel Cody finished his contract for building the present first lock. The old one was torn down and "Vinegar Hill" removed to its present quarters.

In 1824 a small boat, half the size of the common boats of the present day, made regular trips every two hours between Syaracuse and Salina. August Spencer was the first captain of this boat. He was succeeded by Captain William Stewart, the present famous landlord of the Syracuse House. Captain Stewart commanded his boat with great dignity , and treated his passengers with the utmost politeness and attention. The gallant captain exhibited as much pride while pacing the deck of his small craft as of the commanders of the ocean steamers of the present day.

The first horse show was attended by nearly all the citizens, and a full delegation of Onondaga Indians, and Syracuse immediately acquired a reputation as a "good show town", which it has preserved even to the present day.

The first circus that ever performed in Syracuse occupied the vacant lot on the corner of Church and Salina streets, at present occupied by the Onondaga Temperance House.

The success of this circus led to the building of a Circus House in 1825, by Andrew N. VanPatten and John Rogers, on the ground now occupied by the Onondaga Temperance House. This Circus House was subsequently turned into a livery stable with a cooper's shop in the rear, and a long two story building, owned and occupied by Mr. Goings as a carpenter and joiner's shop was erected on the towing path in the rear of the Circus building with an alley of about 25 feet between the buildings.

On the evening of Friday, August 20, 1841, a fire broke out in the carpenter's shop which was occupied by Charles Goings. The building was soon surrounded by a crowd of citizens, using their utmost efforts to extinguish the flames, when suddenly a terrible explosion took place, filling the air with flying cinders, and scattering death and destruction around. This catastrophe was one of the most distressing events that ever occurred in the history of this or any other city, and we have therefore given a very full description of the calamity, copied from the files of the papers of this year:

[From the *Onondaga Standard*]

Fire and Great Loss of Life by the Explosion of Gunpowder

One of the most deeply afflicting events that ever occurred in our town took place last night. At about half past 9 o'clock, the alarm of fire was given, which brought most of our citizens to a wooden building situate on the tow path of the Oswego canal, nearly in rear of the County Clerk's Office, and occupied as a joiner's shop by Charles Goings. At the time we had reached the spot, the roof of the building was completely enveloped in flames. The engine companies were near the fire, and appeared to be doing good execution. Presently we heard the cry of "Powder! Powder! There is powder in the building!" When this cry was given nearly the whole crowd rushed back, but the move was but momentary. Most of those nearest the fire maintained their position, and very few appeared to place an credit in the report. At this time, we were standing within fifty or sixty feet of the flames - the building had been on fire perhaps fifteen minutes - when a tremendous explosion took place, completely checking the fire and demolishing the building. This explosion lasted, we should think, 3 or 4 seconds, filling the air with fragments of the building, and creating the greatest consternation imaginable. The noise of the explosion having ceased, all was still for a moment, and then the most heart rending groans that ever reached our ears were distinctly heard.

The first person we met after the shock was Mr. Myers, the lock tender, a tall, athletic man, with part of his face blown off, and his head and shoulders completely covered with cinders and blood. He begged someone to go home with him, and two persons readily accompanied him. The next was a person brought out dead; one side of his head having been blown off and his brains fallen out. Oh, mercy, what a sight. Then followed other scenes which it is impossible to describe. All was confusion. Although the sight of the dead and the dying was horrible, it was scarcely less than the living inquiring for their relatives - parents for their children and wives, almost frantic with despair, for their husbands.

Everything, we believe, was done that could have been done under the circumstances. An extra train of cars was run to Auburn for physicians, and our hotel keepers threw open their doors for the reception of the wounded. We were on the ground an hour after the explosion occurred and witnessed the greatest kindness on the part of all. Every effort was made to extricate the bodies, and to afford all the consolation and relief that could be afforded.

As to the origin of the fire, it is unknown; but it is supposed that it was the work of an incendiary. The fire appeared to have commenced in the top of the building. The powder - some say 10, others say 15 kegs - was placed on the lower floor, under a work bench, and belonged to Malcolm & Hudson.

Such is a brief and imperfect sketch of this awful calamity - a calamity which, from the carelessness, avarice, or malignity of one or two or three persons, has sent, or probably will send, not less than thirty of their fellow beings into Eternity; and most of them without a moment's warning. What a subject for reflection! Let those who escaped, and we are one among the number - feel grateful to that Good Being, whose ways, though inscrutable, are always just.

Mr. Hudson, firm of Malcolm & Hudson, the owners of the powder, in his testimony before the jury, stated that there were 23 kegs, containing 25 pounds each, and 4 kegs containing 12 1/2 lbs. each, making in all 625 lbs, deposited in the upper story of the building, in the northeast corner, if we recollect rightly, on or about the 12th instant. Had the powder been in the lower story as we first stated, or deposited in the western part of the building, the destruction of lives must have been far greater, as the great majority of people on the ground stood on the western side and were unhurt. Most of those killed were on the eastern side of the building which stood within ten or fifteen feet of the canal. Here the several engine companies stood, the space between the building and the canal scarcely affording then sufficient room to work advantageously.

So great was the force of the explosion on the eastern side of the building that the west side of Dr. Parker's salt block, 100 feet distant, was badly shattered, and a small dwelling the same distance almost torn from its foundation. It was evident that by the location of the powder the principal timbers of the building were thrown in an east and southeasterly direction. The smallest number of persons stood in that direction, and so far as we can learn, few there ever heard the cry of powder, and those who did failed to put much confidence in the report. Mr. Hudson, Mr. Goings and others who knew that there was powder in the building, stated on oath yesterday that they did all they could to spread this information at the time of the fire, it is evident, we think that they scarcely knew what they were about, or that they neglected their duty and are therefore greatly to blame. Such was the force of the concussion that nearly whole windows were broken out of the Mansion House, 100 rods distant. People from the country inform us that the shock was sensibly felt 20 miles distance.

The list we now publish of those killed may be relied upon as correct, it having been furnished us by the coroner. As for the wounded, although we have but 65 names on our list, there must be many more whose names have not been handed in - perhaps not less that 80 or 90 in all, who are more or less hurt.

The funerals of most of those deceased took place this morning, and their bodies being followed to the grave by our citizens, fireman, five companies of fireman from Utica, and a large number of people from the country. Business was completely suspended during the whole of yesterday. Hundreds of people from different parts of the country came to witness the effects of the fire, and altogether our place presented such a scene as we never before witnessed, and we earnestly hope we shall never witness again.

NAMES OF PERSONS KILLED, FURNISHED BY THE CORONER

Thomas Betts, tallow chandler; friends reside in Rochester, aged about 30.
Elijah Jones, carpenter and joiner, man of family, aged 40 yrs., resided in Skaneateles.
Zebina Dwight, kept livery stable, has a wife, aged 30 years.

William Conklin, butcher, single man, aged about 21, has a widowed mother.

Benj. F. Johnson, farmer, aged 17, resided in Florence, Oneida Co.

Elisha Ladd, salt boiler, from Richland, Oswego Co., age 23.

George W. Burdick, canal boat captain, aged 24, has a wife and two children, resided in Clay.

Isaac Stanton, stone cutter, has a marble yard, aged 35, has a wife and two children.

Hugh T. Gibson, salt manufacturer, foreman of Engine No. 3, aged 40 years, has a wife and two children.

William B. Close, cooper, aged 45, has wife and three children.

George Gorman, laborer, aged 35, has wife and three children

Horace T. Goings, carpenter and joiner, age 23.

Charles T. Moffit, clerk for Bradley & Co., aged 34, has wife and two children.

Horatio N. Cheney, weigh master, aged 36, has a wife and three children.

Loren L. Cheney, weigh master's clerk, aged 24.

John Durnford, Jr., attorney at law, aged 23.

Hanson Maynard, clerk for J. M. Richards aged 19.

Noah Hoyt, blacksmith, aged 28

John Kohlhamer, carriage maker, aged 34, has wife and three children.

Matthew Smelt, tailor, employed by Longstreet & Agnew, aged 23.

Ezra H. Hough, druggist, aged 25, parents reside at Summer Hill, Cayuga Co.

James M. Baker, clerk for his father, aged 21.

Charles Miller, carpenter and joiner, aged 20, resides at Pompey

Benjamin T. Baker, aged 16, son of B. Baker.

Charles Austin, aged 16, son of Ezekiel Austin.

WOUNDED DANEROUSLY

David Myers	Elisha George
Z. Robinson	D. C. LeRoy
W. Durant	Luther Gifford
Son of John Thorn	S. W. Cadwell

BADLY

Hugh Rogers
Paul Shaw
J. Goodrich
P. Balin
Thos. R. Hall
E. Morehouse
John McDermott
Patrick Denfee
John Eliker
P. Thurber
John Jones
--- Handwright
L. J. Benton
--- Lucus
Jerry Stevens
Mrs. Appleton

Miss Elliston
Thomas Poe
Myron Jacobs
Son of Peter Lele
Orson Putnam
Elisha Jones
B. L. Higgins
E. Rosebrook
L. W. Bement
George B. Walter
George W. Benedict
Jonathan Baldwin
John McCaslin
Frederick Strongman
Lewis Corbin
--- Lake

SLIGHTLY

William B. Durkee
Richard Culvert
Oliver Drew
Clozen Spencer
John B. Phelps
Dr. James Foran
David Wheeler
Robert Armstrong
Nelson Gilbert
Mr. Martin
John Burns
D. Brown

Lewis Smith
Luke Collins
Henry Hoag
Thomas H. Ostrander
P. Lowe
John Conklin
S. Packwood
J. Crawe
I. D. Lawson
S. Hurst
John Shoins
H. S. Sloan

At a meeting of our citizens, held this afternoon at the Presbyterian Church for the purpose of taking into consideration the proper mode of relieving the necessities of those whose situation may require aid, Hiram Putnam, President of the village, was called to the Chair and D. D. Hillis, Esq., appointed Secretary. After the names of the dead and wounded had been read, and inquiries made relative to the condition of such as stand in need, it was resolved that a committee of five be appointed to ascertain the situation of the sufferers and their families, and to afford them such relief as may be obtained by subscriptions from our citizens. The committee for this village is composed of Daniel Dana, M. D. Burnett, A. P. Granger, Charles L. Lynds, and Wing Russell. For Salina, Ashbel Kellogg and Col. E. D. Hopping.

At the meeting above mentioned, about $1800.00 were subscribed on the spot, of which Malcolm & Hudson subscribed $500.00 and William Malcolm, $500.00.

In consequence of the great and unprecedented loss of life at the fire and explosion of gunpowder in this village, on the night of the 20th of August, inst., Parley Bassett, Esq., the Coroner summoned the following person to form a jury of inquest, to make an inquisition over the bodies of those killed:

Johnson Hall, as Foreman

Pliny Dickinson	Harmon W. VanBuren
Lewis H. Redfield	Daniel Elliott
D. S. Colvin	Ashbel Kellogg
William A. Cook	Thomas G. Alvord
Thomas T. Davis	Elijah W. Curtis
Samuel Larned	Jared H. Parker
Rial Wright	Amos P. Granger
Philo D. Mickles	

The Coronor's Jury closed its business on Monday evening, August 23rd. The report concludes as follows:

That Hugh T. Gibson, Ezra H. Hough, Thomas Betts, Elijah Jones, Zebina Dwight, William Conklin, Benjamin F. Johnson, Elisha Ladd, George W. Burdick, Isaac Stanton, William B. Close, George Gorman, Horace T. Goings, Charles A. Moffit, Loren L. Cheney, Horatio N. Cheney, John Durnford, Jr., Hanson Maynard, Noah Hoyt, Joel Kohlhamer, Matthew Smelt, James M. Barker, Charles Miller, Benjamin T. Baker, Charles Austin, came to their deaths on the night of Friday, the 20th of August, 1841, by the explosion of 27 or 28 kegs of gunpowder in a carpenter's and joiner's shop, then on fire in the village of Syracuse, and which the said deceased and others were attempting to extinguish; that in the belief of the jury , the said shop was set on fire by some person or persons unknown; that the said powder was the property of William Malcolm and Albert H. Hudson of Syracuse, and was secretly stored in the said shop by the said Albert A. Hudson and Charles Goings, the owner of the said shop, with the knowledge and consent of the said William Malcolm, contrary to the published and known ordinances of the village of Syracuse and without the cognizance or consent of the Trustees thereof.

[From the *Western State Journal*]
THE AWFUL CATASTROPHE OF FRIDAY NIGHT

We cannot yet scarcely realize the scenes of this dreadful night. They seem to us like the delusive dreams of a disordered imagination. We cannot bring our sober thoughts to reflect that so many with whom we had daily and some almost hourly intercourse - who were on the ill-fated evening in high spirits, buoyant with strong hopes and long lives - have been cut off thus prematurely without a second's warning.

The effects of the explosion were felt for over twenty miles around us. A man upon the deck of a packet boat at Fulton, 26 miles distant, heard the report. At DeWitt and Jamesville, five miles off, persons were startled from their sleep, supposing that their chimneys had fallen down. A number got up and went out door to examine their houses. At Camillus, about the same distance west of us, it appeared like a falling of a tree against the house with a scraping downwards. A merchant in Manlius, eight miles, says that the crockery rattled in his store, as though a tremendous thunder clap had broken over it. At Onondaga, on high ground, 4 and 6 miles, many supposed it to be an earthquake, the house shook so. Here, although the concussion was tremendous in the vicinity, the report was not so loud as might have been expected - perhaps not louder than a 32 or 40 pounder. The glass in windows 80 or 100 rods were many of them broken. Many of the papers in the County Clerk's office, directly west, were thrown out of their places upon the floor. Dr. J. H. Parker's salt block, on the heel path, directly east was very much injured, the sides and roof are shattered and broken in. Pieces of the building three or four feet long were driven through the side entirely into the salt. Dr. P. and his wife were standing in front of his salt works at the time of the explosion. They were both knocked down, but not seriously injured. Smelt, a worthy young man, a tailor, Ladd a salt boiler and another young man were killed by their side, and Hough and Kohlhamer were blown nearly across there also.

The instant the explosion took place the air was filled with missiles and fragments of the building, staves and lumber, which lit up the heavens with brightness, but in a moment it was total darkness. The explosion had extinguished every particle of fire. The scene that was then presented was horrible beyond description. Amidst the darkness the groans of the dying and wounded, the stumbling over the mutilated bodies, the weeping of friends and relatives, the heart of man was completely overpowered. We have never imagined anything of the tragic and horrible to be compared to it. The greatest confusion followed. Some 2000 or 3000 inhabitants were soon drawn together, all looking after friends. Very soon lamps were brought, the wounded were carried off, groaning continually; the dead were examined, and perhaps a dear son, the pride and ornament of the family circle, was discovered, mangled and disfigured so that he could only be recognized by his hair, the contents of his pockets or his clothing. Then a father would be taken up, whose distracted widow would be waiting in the vicinity to know the worst. And so it continued for hours, until the canal had been drained, and a number of bodies taken from thence. Clumps of persons with lights could be seen in all directions carrying either their dead or the wounded to their homes. The scenes of this night will long be remembered by the people of Syracuse. Sadness pervaded every building and melancholy regrets every heart.

As soon after the catastrophe as the senses of our citizens could be gathered, expresses were sent in all direction of the country for physicians and surgeons. The Syracuse & Auburn Railroad Co. ran an extra train to Auburn for the same purpose. The professional gentlemen obeyed the summons with alacrity and were soon here beside the beds of the wounded. All that could be done was accomplished and the unfortunates were made as comfortable as possible. The weather taking a favorable turn, and becoming cooler, added very much to the comfort of the sufferers.

On Saturday the village was shrouded in mounring. The stores were all closed. Business was out of the question. Hundreds of people from the country towns came hurrying in, on learning the awful intelligence, to see the spot so fruitful with distress, and to know the minutiae of the sad affair.

Sunday was a busy day entombing the dead. The cars from the east brought some five fire companies, dressed in uniform, from Utica. A western train brough a number of Auburn people, and the people from the county came in again - all to mingle their tears and sympathies with those of this afflicted community.

Early in the day the funeral processions commenced from different directions, and from the several churches, and there was one continual successions of corses [sic] passing to the lonely sepulchre. The two Cheneys were laid side by side in one common grave. The graveyard appears full of fresh mounds. Over twenty are fresh, and will remain so in the remembrance of thousands for a long time to come.

The several churches were crowded, The clergmen were most solemn and impassioned in their addresses. A deeper sadness never pervaded so large a congregation . Many of those present were standing beside those on Friday night who were cut down like grass, and are now in eternity. The living felt most devoutly thankful for the mercy of God shown in their deliverance. Women who had husbands and sons there, praised their Heavenly Father that they were not made widows and childless in the sad havoc of young and old.

SOUTH SIDE ERIE CANAL

On the corner now occupied by Messrs. Stone & Ball, jewelers, and Messrs. Sabey & Weaver, there stood in 1824 a two story frame building, known as the "Coffin Block." The name was given to the block on account of its fancied resemblance to that receptacle for the dead. The first and second stories on the extreme corner were then occupied by John Durnford, Esq., as a book store, lottery ticket office and printing office.

From this corner the first number of the *Onondaga Gazette,* the first paper ever issued in this city was printed by John Durnford, our present worthy Justice of the Peace. The first number was issued Wednesday morning, April 2, 1823. In his "Address" to the public, the publisher lays down the following views and principles:

"Notwithstanding it may be said the state already abounds with newspapers, yet the rapid growth of the country, and the happy location of this village, in connection with its other advantages are sufficient to warrant the belief that ere long Syracuse and its vicinity will afford and adequate support to this establishment, and raise up a monumental trophy of the wisdom and enterprise of the canal projectors.

"Allied to no party, this paper will be independent in politics - mild, but when necessary, decisive - supporting the authorities of both State and Nation - advocating the people's cause, and recommending such men for public favor as may be entitled to it by their talents and integrity. And it ought to be remembered while enjoying the blessing of freedom and independence, the only way to secure these blessing is to encourage virtue, and suppress vice, by exciting a laudable ambition in those who aspire for popular distinction, to have a good character - the surest recommendation."

The terms of the paper were, "to village subscribers who receive the paper at their dwellings, $2.50, payable half yearly.

To single subscribers in the vicinity of the village, who take their paper from the office, $2.00 payable as above.

To mail subscribers, $2.00 payable in advance.

To good responsible post riders, a liberal deduction will be made, and no paper discontinued until all arrearages are paid, but at the discretion of the publisher.

The *Gazette* was a weekly paper published on a 12 x 17 sheet, four pages, with five columns to the page. The first number contained a number of well selected miscellaneous articles of prose and poetry, the latest news from Europe, bearing date Liverpool,

Feb. 1, 1823 which announced the declaration of War by France upon Spain... It contained an account of a large fire in Philadelphia, and various rumors of news and interest clipped from contemporary papers of the day, together with an account of a meeting held in Salina. It also contained a long advertisement of "Pomeroy's Metallic Strop and Paste," Clark's Commentary on the Old and New Testament," "New York Bank Exchange," ...An advertisement of "Morse's Universal Geography," an "Apprentice to the printing business wanted," Kasson's and Heermans' advertisement of "Dry Goods, Groceries, Crockery & Hardware," "Dr. Lee's Genuine Windham Bilious Pills," "Cash Paid For Rags," "Wanted, an apprentice to the tailoring business," and the advertisement of "James Anti-Dyspeptic Pills".

It also contained a call for a meeting of the "Onondaga Salt Co., Stephen Smith, Sec'y," and the "List of Letters remaining in the Postoffice at Syracuse, April 1, 1823", John Wilkinson Postmaster. The list consisted of the names of eight persons, and occupied a half square in the paper.

The first number also contained the notice of death at Washington of the Hon. Brouckholst Livingston, one of the Associate Justices of the Supreme Court...in the 66th year of his age.

On the 31st of Mar. 1824, the paper appeared under the name of the *Syracuse Gazette*. The *Syracuse Gazette* was published by Mr. Durnford until 1829 when Lewis H. Redfield, of the *Onondaga Register*, then published in Onondaga Hollow, came to Syracuse, bought out Mr. Durnford, and united the two papers under the name of *The Syracuse Gazette and Onondaga Register*. He continued to publish this paper until 1831, when it was transferred to other hands.

In 1824, Henry W. Durnford occupied the first store east of the *Syracuse Gazette* office, as a drug store. He also kept an assortment of groceries, crockery, and liquors, and transacted a large and profitable business.

That year it was deemed necessary for the convenience of the public to remove the Postoffice, then under the charge of John Wilkinson, to some more convenient location than General Granger's store. Mr. Wilkinson made selection of Mr. Durnford's store as the location for the new Postoffice and consulted with him in regard to the matter. Mr. Durnford raised the objection of a "lack of room" for all the purposes of the Postoffice. Mr. Wilkinson thought different, and to convince the incredulous storekeeper, crossed the canal and returned bearing the whole Postoffice, boxes, mail bags, mail matter, and all appurtenances on his shoulders. This feat convinced Mr. Durnford that he had plenty of room in which to accommodate the Post Office.

The first store east of the drug store was occupied by John Rodgers & Co. as a dry goods store. Mr. Rodgers was an energetic, enterprising man, and is now one of the millionaires of Chicago, and visits the scene of his early prosperity yearly.

Between the store of Mr. Rodgers and the drug store there was a wide hall-like entrance leading to the printing office in the second story, and the rooms occupied as a dwelling by Mr. VanVelzer.

Gen. Jonas Mann began in 1824 to build a store on the corner now occupied by the bookstore of Peck & Rudd. He also commenced to build a dwelling house the present famous "Cook's Coffee House." He moved his family here the next season, and during the summer finished both buildings.

Henry Newton occupied the first store east of Mr. Mann's building as a grocery and general assortment store. Mr. Newton afterwards formed a partnership with A. Root, in the boot and shoe business on the north side of the canal.

Joseph Slocum carried on the dry goods business, and also kept a general assortment of wares and merchandise, next east of Mr. Newton's grocery.

A. N. VanPatten carried on the dry goods, grocery and provision business in the first store east of Mr. Slocum's grocery. Over the store a man by the name of Thompson kept a billiard table during the fall and winter.

Deacon Phelps kept a stove store and grocery on the first floor, and a tin shop in the second story of the first building east of Mr. VanPatton's store. Between the tinshop and Warren street, there were a series of vacant lots. These lots were subsequently occupied by fine blocks and stores. In 1834 they were all reduced to a heap of smoldering ruins. The burning of these two blocks, comprising ten buildings of different dimensions, with eleven buildings on the north side of the canal, was the first great calamity that ever befell the embryo city. The following *Onondaga Standard Extra* was issued on the evening after the frightful occurrence. We give it entire:

About 11:00 last evening a fire broke out in the store of B. F. Rodgers, nearly opposite the Syracuse House. It spread rapidly along in both directions, and in a short time the whole line of buildings on both sides of the canal , from the public Square east, as far as Warren Street were in flames and are now a heap of ruins! ! Ten buildings on the south side of the canal were burned. Of these five were of brick three or four stories in height, The Syracuse House was saved by the greatest exertions. The east wing containing the Onondaga County Bank was several times on fire.

Eleven building were consumed on the north side of the canal. The buildings consumed were all occupied as stores, offices, and shops and were all among the most important places of business.

The printing establishment of this paper was nearly, and that of the *Constitutional* entirely destroyed.

We shall continue the publication of the *Standard,* but must for a short item ask the indulgence of our patrons, while it may be necessary to publish it in a reduced form until our office can be re-established.

The loss sustained by this dreadful fire cannot be less than $75,000, of which we understand one-half was insured. The whole number of persons in business, in the blocks destroyed and who have suffered, is over fifty, among whom are many cases of sever loss.

On the corner now occupied by Murphy, McCarthy and Co., hardware dealers, John Rodgers carried on in 1824 the storage, forwarding and commission business in connection with his Dry Goods Store. The building was burned down afterward.

Messrs. White & Clark occupied the first store east, and dealt in all descriptions of merchandise and produce. They were also engaged in the storage and commission business in the building standing next east of their store.

Joseph Slocum occupied the first building east of White & Clark's storehouse, and carried on a general storage and commission business.

There was but one other building then standing between Mr Slocum's storehouse and the old canal basin. It was a little low frame building partly hid by the bushes that grew in great profusion in that region. Mr. Joseph Thompson kept a small grocery in the building and derived most of his custom from the canal boatmen by furnishing them with "supplies." In 1824, the present site of the Weigh Lock Market Hall, Hay Market and public square, as far south as the railroad, there formed what was known as the canal basin. It was a miserable, nasty hole, and was the dread of all the inhabitants, because it tainted and infected the whole atmosphere with disease. A small barn stood on the south side of this basin with a path on one side leading into it, which was used as a watering place for cattle and Horses.

In 1824 Parley Howlett and Barney Filkins built a slaughter house on the ground, and the same house is at present occupied by Joe Tasker's well known cottage.

Water street east of the basin had been laid off as a street, but has not been worked to any extent. A few trees and a quantity of underbrush had been cut and a few rails laid in the worst miring places, so that by dint of hard work and hard swearing a team could be got through to old Mr. Russell's pottery. This pottery stood on the ground now occupied by James L. Greenman, storage and commission house. It was carried on by an old man named Russell, who manufactured jars, mugs, jugs, milk pans and all other articles commonly made at such establishments. He resided in a small frame house a little south of his pottery.

Mulberry street was almost impassable for teams in 1824, the ground being very low and marshy in that section.

The State owned a small frame house on the heel path side of the old first lock, which was known and used as a lock house. The building is now standing and forms part of Hatch, Rust & Randall's lumber and coal office.

In 1824 all that portion of our city lying between Mulberry street and Lodi on the south side of the canal was an unreclaimed cedar swamp. The present Fayette Park, with the splendid residences of our merchants and business men, was then a favorite resort for foxes, rabbits and wild fowl, forming a capital shooting ground. North and east of the Park the sonorous croakings of the bull frog serve to enliven the otherwise dismal scenery. This swamp was full of rotten logs and stumps from which issued a deadly miasma containing the whole list of fevers, from fever and ague to the typhoid and brain fever.

The Genesee Turnpike passed through this swamp, and consisted of an ill laid corduroy road that tested the strength of horses and wagons and the skill and moral training of all teamsters having occasion to pass it.

Capt. Oliver Teall owned and ran two small saw mills on the north side of the Erie canal, near the Lodi locks. He obtained the water which moved the mills by tapping the canal. He was then Canal Superintendent under Henry Seymour, Canal Commissioner, and obtained the right to use the water for running his mills from the State.

It was this successful tapping of the great "Clinton Ditch" that gave the well known captain such a decided partiality to cold water over other fluids. It was this very tapping of the Erie which led him to conceive and carry out the grand idea of tapping mother earth, filling a huge reservoir with the crystal nectar and forcing it through great iron arteries and veins to the very heart and extremities of our flourishing city.

The Captain lived in a small house built by the State for a lock house. There were about a dozen little houses scattered about the locks and occupied by the employees on the locks and the canal.

John H. Lathrop kept a tavern in a medium sized house, standing on the block lying southeast of the Orphan Asylum, on the Genesee Turnpike. He had a fine well on his premises affording the best water in the country. People coming from the east to trade or barter in Syracuse would stop with Mr. Lathrop, and from his house go to the village and trade during the day, returning as the shades of evening fell on the gloomy swamp, to his house for food and lodging. They did this instead of putting up at one of the village taverns and running the risk of ague.

At that time Syracuse was considered as the most unhealthy spot in the valley, and people were inclined to believe that the city would be built on the Lodi hills in preference to the middle of a cedar swamp. But the projectors and proprietors of the embryo city did not waver even for an instant, in their choice of location for the village. The present large, flourishing, healthy, wealthy city is the reward of their judgement and faith.

The "Holden House" stood nearly opposite Mr. Lathrop's tavern, and was then used as a dwelling.

At the foot of the hill, near the swamp, on the Genesee Turnpike, Lemuel J. Benton commenced in 1825, to manufacture brick. Henry Shattuck, the present policeman, and Abner Chapman, Supervisor from Onondaga, worked as molders in this brick yard.

Coming west from the brick yard, the mind's eye found nothing to remember, nothing to describe, but a low, sickly cedar swamp and corduroy road, until you reached what now forms the a large part of the heart of our city.

This swamp was the fear of all the inhabitants, and the dread of all in search of a location for a future residence. But the art of man has reclaimed the "Dismal Swamp" and it now forms one of the most beautiful and healthy sections of the city.

Samuel Phelps kept a blacksmith shop on the lot now occupied by the Home Association. The shop was in a two story building, with the front towards Genesee street. The second story, Mr. Phelps occupied as a dwelling. The family reached their rooms by means of an outside pair of stairs. The ground upon which the shop stood was so low and marshy that the fall rains made a large pond all around the building. In the winter this pond formed a famous skating ground for the boys of the village.

In 1824 the remains of a small log house formerly standing on the southwest corner of Genesee and Montgomery streets was visible . In this house Albion Jackson was born about the year 1802. Mr. Jackson was the first white child born within the limits of this city. Shortly after his birth Mr. Jackson's father moved to Canada and was gone some eighteen years before he returned.

The ground upon which the Granger Block now stands was, in 1824, a fine little green meadow. That year Messrs. John Durnford, Archy Kasson and John Rodgers were appointed a committee by the Episcopal Society, authorized and empowered to select a site for a church edifice. Mr. Durnford advocated the selection of this meadow as the proposed site. The other members of the committee offered an objection to the lot "that was too far from the village," but finally coincided with Mr. Durnford in his choice, and the committee reported accordingly.

The report was adopted and immediate measures taken to erect the necessary building. Deacon Wright obtained the contract for performing the carpenter work, and assumed the general superintendence of putting up the building. The building was completed in the year 1825. It was used a number of years by the Episcopalians and then sold to the Roman Catholics who removed it to the corner of Montgomery and Madison streets where it is still standing.

The millinery store of Mrs. Gillmore was erected in 1824 by John Rodgers, then one of the most enterprising men in the village. The mason work was performed by a man from Manlius named Dwinelle.

On the ground now occupied by the Bastable Block there stood in 1824 a little frame house occupied by Mr. Walker. These were the only buildings then standing on the block opposite the Granger Block.

A small yellow building was then standing next east of "Cook's Coffee House" which has since been moved back and a brick from built to it.

Henry Van Husen owned an occupied a blacksmith shop on the corner of Genesee and Warren streets, where the Tremont House now stands. His shop was a hard looking concern and was not much of an ornament to the village even in those primitive days. The building stood about a foot and a half below the level of the mud sidewalk. His customers used to complain of the distance to be traveled and the great depth of mud to be waded through before his shop could be reached from the village. In rainy weather it was almost impossible to reach his shop on account of the mud.

The street and square were then some four feet lower than at the present day and formed one of the worst roads for the passage of teams that can be imagined. I have frequently seem teams with an ordinary load get set in the deep mud and remain some time before they could be extricated.

Harry Durnford resided in a small white house on the ground mow occupied by Gay's Hotel. The house fronted the south. He had a white fence around his lot, and a beautiful flower garden in front of the house. It was a very pretty, cozy little dwelling.

About the year 1820 Messrs. Buel & Safford purchased the ground now occupied by the Syracuse House and commenced construction of the Syracuse Hotel. During the progress of the building Mr. Safford fell from the scaffolding and was killed. The accident caused a temporary suspension of the work, until the property went into the possession of Mr. Eckford, who completed the building in 1822.

The building was of brick, three stories in height, fifty feet square, with a roof pitching north and south with brick battlement on the east and west ends of the upper brake. The front entrance was through the present show store of T. Ryan.

The stables stood well back from Genesee street extending nearly to the present railroad depot. There was a large yard attached to the house and stables in which stood a number of old, dilapidated out buildings. The entrance to the yard was through a large gateway, then standing on the present site of Butler, Townsend & Co's dry goods store.

After the premises fell into the hands of the Syracuse Company they were rebuilt and named the "Syracuse House". The original building has since been enlarged and improved and is now one of the best hotels in this region. James Mann was the landlord of the Syracuse Hotel, which was then the headquarters of the different line of stages.

In 1824 Jason C. Woodruff drove stage between Elbridge and this place. He performed the duties of his office with great dignity, and was wont to wheel his favorite coach up to the door of the Syracuse Hotel with an exhibition of great skill and training. From the post of driver, Mr. Woodruff, by his own unaided exertions, raised himself into the position of proprietor of a line of stages, and has since filled several office of trust and honor in the county, with credit to himself and satisfaction of his fellow citizens.

Col. Elijah Phillips had his stage office in an east room of the Syracuse Hotel. The Colonel was very prompt and exact in his business operations, and for years a stage never drew up to his office without finding him ready to give or receive the way bill. It was a common expression in those days, "Time and Col. Phillips wait for no man."

Next east of the gate leading to the stables of the Syracuse House, a man named Waterbury owned a small frame building. On the first floor he kept a little grocery. His stock in trade consisted of a small quantity of poor whiskey, a few plugs of tobacco, a handful of pipes, and about 88 cents worth of comic valentines. His family lived in the second story, and reached their place of residence by means of a flight of stairs built on the outside of the building.

Next east of Waterbury's there was standing a two-story building, considerably larger than its western neighbor. The first floor was occupied as a dwelling house. The second story was occupied by Mr. Jabez Hawley as a chair factory. These old buildings were rather unprepossessing in their appearance, being a dirty wood color, from having never made the improving acquaintance of a paint pot or brush.

A small house stood next east of Mr. Hawley's shop, which was occupied by a person whose name is forgotten, as a grocery and drinking house. It was originally painted white but the color had worn off and in 1824 the house had a forlorn and dingy appearance. Between this house and the blacksmith shop on the corner of Warren and Genesee streets the ground was vacant.

Archy Kasson built a dwelling house in 1824 on the ground now occupied by the central Railroad Company's ticket office.

The square upon which now stands the Onondaga County Bank, Bank of Syracuse, Dillaye Block, Episcopal Church, and St. Charles Hotel, was in 1824 a vacant lot covered with a few scattered trees.

In 1825 the "First Presbyterian Society of Syracuse" built a church on the ground now occupied by the new and beautiful Dillaye Black. The church was finished in the fall and dedicated in January 1826. The original church was enlarged and improved several years ago but in 1849, the increasing demands of the Society rendered it necessary to build a new edifice. It was accordingly sold, and the present ornament to the city erected in 1850.

The Rev. Dr. John W. Adams was ordained and installed pastor of the new church in June 1826. Dr. Adams continued to act in that capacity until death claimed him as his own in 1850. The reverend doctor was a very exemplary man. He centered and united the affections of this whole about his great heart, and died after a long life of usefulness and devotion to God, deeply mourned by all who ever had the pleasure and profit of his acquaintance.

The entire square, with the exception of the church lot, was afterwards offered to the county free of charge, if the supervisors would agree to build a court house and jail upon it. After some deliberations on the matter the offer was refused by the board.

A small unpainted house with an L, stood nearly on the present site of the Washington block. The main part of this house was occupied by Widow Stewart, and the L by Mr. Wheeler. Mrs. Stewart is the mother-in-law of John Hurst, Esq., our worthy Justice of the Peace. She is now over eighty years of age, straight and active as a girl of eighteen. She was one of the early settlers of this county, and formerly lived in Liverpool.

A farm belonging to the Syracuse Co. and occupied by Jacob Hausenfrats, stood on the present site of Capt. Thomas Wheeler's residence, on what was then a little knoll. The barn stood on the ground now occupied by the residence of William B. Kirk, and a corn house stood a little east of the dwelling. Mr. Hausenfrats worked the farm on shares for the Company, and a had a large wheat field extending from the First Methodist Church west nearly on the line of Jefferson street to his house.

Between the house and village a small brook called Yellow Brook, ran from the swamp and emptied into the old millpond. The passage of water through this brook had cut a ravine over fifteen feet deep where it crossed Salina street. Previous to 1824 there was a bridge across this brook on Salina street, but by means of a sluice the ravine had been partly filled up and the bridge removed. All south of the wheat field was a young unclaimed forest, thickly overgrown with underbrush.

Zophar Adams manufactured brick in 1824 on the west side of Salina street, a little south of the farmhouse. I think Dr. Westcott's residence stands on the ground then used as a brick yard.

South Salina street was then a full six feet higher than at the present day, and very irregular, passing over a series of mounds or hillocks the whole distance, making a bad road to travel with a loaded team.

That portion of the city now known as Onondaga street or Cinder road, was in 1824 a cedar swamp, with a quantity of old logs, stumps and trunks of fallen trees slowly going to decay, and filling the air with noxious vapors. Wherever the land was sufficiently firm and dry to afford soil, there a very luxuriant growth of blackberry bushes had sprung up, yielding innumerable quarts of that delicious fruit.

This swamp was also a great resort for game, and has been the scene of many hunting and blackberrying adventures to the children of larger growth as well as to the youth of Syracuse and vicinity. The swamp extended from the pond as far as Col. Johnson's present residence.

That year [1824] the proprietor of Mickles' Furnace generously appropriated the cinders formed by this furnace to filling up a road through the swamp. A cart with two horses driven tandem, and a man to load, drive and deposit the cinders was furnished by the Syracuse Co. and the drawing of cinders was continued until a coat of them had been placed on the road a foot and a half thick. This gave it the name of Cinder road which it has ever since retained.

A man named Finch lived in a small log house near the reservoir on the Cinder road. This man was very dissipated and finally died in that house. Thurlow Weed's father lived, previous to 1824, on the Cinder road near Col. Johnson's, in a small log house.

The canal basin between Salina and Clinton streets was not as large in 1824 as at the present time. It was so narrow as scarcely to afford turning room for even the small boats used in those days. When an extra amount of water was let into the canal the banks of the basin were frequently overflowed and the cellars in the vicinity filled with water.

A small footbridge with stairs on each end spanned the canal several yards east of the resent Clinton street bridge. At the foot of this bridge on the southeast side Deacon Chamberlain, father-in-law of Ex-Mayor Stevens, kept a meat market in a small frame building painted yellow.

Hiram Hyde kept two store houses adjoining each other on the ground now occupied by the old Raynor block, a little west of the Clinton street bridge. Mr. Hyde was a son-in-law of Joshua Forman, and a man of enterprise and integrity. He died in 1825 of consumption.

There were no other buildings on the north side of Water street between Salina and Onondaga Creek.

LeGrand and William Crofoot carried on the manufacture of brick on the ground at present occupied by Greenway's malt house on West Water street.

In the spring of 1824 Messrs. Kasson & Heermans carried on the hardware business in a small wooden building and erected a three story brick block seventy feet deep. The building was afterwards occupied by Messrs. Horace and Charles Wheaton, as a hardware store and in 1849 it was destroyed by fire, together with a long row of small wooden buildings extending nearly to the Townsend block.

Weiting block and hall was erected and finished during the years 1849-50. On the 5th of Jan. 1856, one of the coldest days during the winter, this beautiful block was burned to the ground. Dr. Weiting at once took measures for erection of a new block, if possible larger, better and more beautiful than the former one.

Cheney & Wilcox obtained the contract for performing the mason work on the building. Under their combined efforts and the superintending eyes of Dr. Wieting and H. N. White, the architect, the building rose like a Phoenix from the ashes, larger better and more substantial and more beautiful than the former splendid block.

The new hall is one of the best in the state and is not excelled out of New York in point of convenience and beauty. The Doctor deserves credit for his unremitting exertions and expenditure of money. The new hall was dedicated on the 9th of December 1856, eleven months from the date of the destruction of the former building.

In the summer of 1824, William Malcolm put up a frame building on the ground now forming the center of the Wieting block on Water street. He occupied this building the following spring as a hardware store. Mr. Malcolm also built a dwelling house on the present site of the Malcolm block.

The Syracuse Co. put up three or four small wooden buildings west of Malcolm's which they let to different persons as stores and groceries.

Moses D. Burnet occupied the small frame building standing a little west of the company's store as an office. A large hickory tree stood in front of this office affording a fine shade. The Major was an energetic and enterprising man, and in the spring of 1824 was appointed the agent of the Syracuse Co. He has since occupied several offices of profit and trust with ability and success. He was once elected mayor of the city but refused to serve. The Major is a whole-souled man and is now quietly enjoying the rewards of his early labors.

Ambrose Kasson lived in a small frame house standing a little west of Major Burnett's office. John Durnford occupied a dwelling west of Mr. Kasson's. The two houses had very pretty yards in front, filled with flower beds and shrubbery.

Dr. M. Williams came to this place in 1824 and established himself in the practice of medicine. The Doctor, for some months, kept his office in the front room over Gen. Granger's store and boarded with him. Then he moved to Forman's office and boarded in his family. He subsequently became the son-in-law of Judge Forman.

The Doctor was a hard working, go-ahead man and by his influence contributed greatly to the prosperity of the embryo city. The village was known throughout the country as a most un-healthy locality. The Doctor combatted the idea with all his power, claiming that the day was not far distant when the village would be a "city of refuge" for consumptive patients. The prediction, to our knowledge has proved true in a large number of cases and we can safely claim that Syracuse is one of the most healthy localities in the state. Dr. Williams of today is the Dr. Williams of 1824 in dress and personal appearance. He does not appear to change or grow old in the least.

Clinton street was not passable for teams in 1824.

Judge Joshua Forman moved to this place in the fall of 1819 and occupied the dwelling house now standing next west of the "Climax House" on Water street. In 1824 he was still living in the same house and had a large garden extending from Clinton street down Water street, to Franklin street, and back to Fayette street. The garden was well stocked with fruit and was tended by a protestant Irishman, named Montgomery; a very intelligent, faithful man.

The Judge was the father of the canal and of Syracuse. Col. Stone, formerly editor of the New York Commercial Advertiser, in giving an account of a western journey, compares Syracuse in 1820 with Syracuse in 1840 in the following language: "Mr. Forman, in one sense was the father of the canal. That is, being a member of the Legislature in 1807, he moved the first resolution of inquiry upon the subject of opening a channel of artificial navigation from the Hudson river to the great lakes. And from that day to the completion of the stupendous work in 1825, his exertions were unremitting and powerful in the cause. Passing as the canal does close by the head of Onondaga Lake, within a toss of a biscuit of some of the salt springs, and within two miles of the principal and strongest fountain at Salina, Mr. Forman saw the immense advantages which the site of this place presented for a town; with the completion of the middle section of the canal Syracuse was begun. At the period of my first visit but a few scattered and indifferent houses had been erected amid the stumps of the recently felled trees. I lodged for a night at a miserable tavern, thronged by a company of salt boilers from Salina, forming a group about as rough looking specimens of humanity as I had ever seen. Their wild visages, beard thick and long, matted hair, even now rise up in dark distant and picturesque perspective before me. I passed a restless night, disturbed by strange fancies, as I yet well remember. It was in October and a flurry of snow during the night had rendered the morning aspect of the country more dreary than the evening before. The few houses I have already described, standing on low and marshy ground, and surrounded by trees and entangled thickets, presented a very uninviting scene. 'Mr Forman' I said, 'do you call this a village? It would make an owl weep to fly over it.' 'Never mind' said he in reply, 'you will live to see it a city yet.

"These words were prophetical. The contrast between the appearance of the town then and now is wonderful. A city it now in extent, and the magnitude and durability of its dwellings.

As I glanced upward and around upon the splendid hotels, rows of massive buildings in all directions, and lofty spires of churches glittering in the sun, and traversed the extended and well-built streets, thronged with people full of life and activity - the canal basins crowded with boat lading and unlading at the large and lofty stone warehouses upon the wharves - the change seemed like one of enchantment."

Judge Forman went to Washington to see Thomas Jefferson in regard to the canal, but did not meet with success, that great statesman remarking, "You are a hundred years too soon with your project." The Judge met and overcame all obstacles in his project of building a city at this point, and so long as Syracuse preserves a place in the list of cities, Joshua Forman will be known and honored by its inhabitants.

Judge Webb built the stone house lately used as a United States recruiting office, on Water street, in 1824, and occupied it as a dwelling house.

The first burying ground in Syracuse comprised a little knoll on Fayette street, near its junction with Clinton street. Fifteen or twenty persons were buried there, and their bodies have never been removed. Thousands are constantly passing over the ground, wholly unconscious that they are passing over the last resting place of those who once as proudly trod the soil of Syracuse.

The old burying ground on Water and Fayette streets was laid out in 1819 by John Wilkinson, and Owen Forman, at the same time they laid out the "Walton Tract", into village lots.

The first person buried there was the wife of Deacon Spencer, sister of G.B. Fish, of this city. The second person buried there was a Mr. West, a circus rider, who was killed by a fall in the old circus house.

The old log dam across the creek on Water street was removed in 1824, and a large stone one erected in its place. The dam stood where Water street bridge now crossed the creek. The pond extended over a great extent of the country, running up to the then new cemetery, up Fayette street, to the old cemetery, and up Clinton street to the Cinder road. In 1849 this pond was filled up by earth conveyed from Prospect hill, and the great cause of sickness and death in our city was effectually removed. The ground thus made is now partly occupied by the freight depot, and works of the Binghamton Railroad, the coal yards of Messrs. Cobb and Hatch, Rust & Co., the residence of Jason C. Woodruff, and a number of other buildings.

An old saw mill, pretty much used up, stood a little east of the stone mill, and was run by Maron Lee as sawyer.

The stone mill was built in 1825, by Samuel Booth, for the Syracuse Company.

A man named Clapp, familiarly known as "Old Sandy," lived in the swamp on the ground at present covered by the round house of the Central Railroad Company. He was a very eccentric man.

The rest of the country west of the creek was a swamp full of rotten logs, stumps, brush, etc., the fear of all the inhabitants.

James Pease came here in 1824, from Lyons, by the canal, and brought a small frame house on a boat, which he put up on the ground now occupied by the Mechanics' bank. In this house Mr. Pease manufactured and sold boots and shoes for many years. He was a very exemplary man, and was liked and respected by the whole village.

In 1824 an alley was by common consent, left open between Kasson & Co.'s hardware store, on the corner, and Mr. Pease's shop for the purpose of allowing teams to pass to the rear of the stores fronting on Water street. This alley was to remain open forever, but it is now covered by one of Dr. Wieting's splendid stores.

In 1824 Theodore Ashley bought out a man named Kneeland, who kept a chair factory next south of James Pease's shoe shop. Mr. Ashley entered into the manufacture of chairs and cabinet ware, and continued in the same business until the time of his death in 1855. Mr. Ashley was a prompt business man and fair in his dealings. He was for several years city sexton, and died regretted by a large circle of friends and acquaintances.

There was standing in 1824 on the ground now covered by the Syracuse City Bank, an old frame building occupied for various purposes. In 1828 Grove Lawrence removed this building, and erected instead a fine brick block.

In 1819 John Wilkinson, in company with Owen Forman, a brother of the Judge, came here from Onondaga Hollow, and under the direction of Judge Forman proceeded to lay out the "Walton Tract" into village lots. This survey was not accomplished without the severest labor. The old lines and marks of the tract were nearly obliterated, and it was with the greatest difficulty that they found with any degree of certainty the starting point of the original survey. The survey was completed after several weeks of hard labor. Part of the "Walton Tract" was laid out into village lots, and the remainder into farm lots of from five to ten acres. After completing the survey Mr. Wilkinson built an office on the corner now occupied by the Globe hotel, and commenced the practice of law. The office was a small one, being but twelve by fourteen, and Mr. Wilkinson was heartily ridiculed for putting his office out in the fields. That location, now forming the business center of our flourishing city, was then out of town.

In February, 1820, a post office was established in Syracuse and Mr. Wilkinson was appointed postmaster. In May, 1825 when the first election for village officers was held, Mr. Wilkinson was elected clerk.

Mr. Wilkinson has since held several offices of profit and trust with honor and distinction. When railroads were first successfully put in operation Mr. Wilkinson closely investigated their workings and principles and his giant mind comprehending the advantages, and ultimate supercedence over the common post roads, he entered at once largely into railroad affairs and is now emphatically a Railroad King.

He was for several years president of the Syracuse & Utica road, and by his influence succeeded in having the workshops of that road built at Syracuse, thus adding the hardy population of the fifth ward to our city. He is now the president of the Michigan Southern road, and under his skillful management that road is one of the best in the Union. Mr. Wilkinson is a great favorite with the traveling public, and is loved and respected by all railroad men, who would do anything for him.

In 1824 Mr. Wilkinson built a residence a little southwest of his office, where he resided a number of years. He now lives in one of the most beautiful palaces on James street.

Mr. Heermans built a house a little south of Mr. Wilkinson's, which he occupied as a dwelling for a number of years.

The Syracuse Company built a frame house in 1824 on the ground at present covered by D. McCarthy & Co.'s mammoth stores.

Kirk's Tavern was built by John Garrison in 1824. The house is now standing, and is kept by E.G. Smith. At the time it was built the mud on Salina street was hardly wadeable. Overshoes were of no account in those days, and boots were hardly a protection against the mud and water. Mechanics at work in the village refused to board there, giving as a reason that the house was so far out from the main village, and the street was so muddy they could not get their meals.

Mr. Kirk came here in 1826 and opened a house as a tavern. He was for a number of years the sole proprietor, and enjoyed the reputation of being a first class landlord. He was a favorite with the country people and his house was always filled with them. He retired from active life several years ago, and is now quietly enjoying his well earned riches. None know him but love and respect him.

A man named White built a small frame house on the ground now occupied by the Gothic house a little south of the Pike Block. There were no other buildings on the south side of the canal in 1824.

Salina street, from the canal to Fayette street was then from three to four feet lower than at the present day, and during the spring and fall it was nearly impassable from the depth of mud. There were no sidewalks, and pedestrians were compelled to pick their way along the street as best they could. Teams would frequently get set in the mud and require great exertions to extricate them. This portion of the street has since been filled up, and the southern portion been cut down to its present level.

The land west of Salina street was then covered with scattered pine trees, oak underbrush, fallen logs, and old stumps, dow to the creek and pond which have all long since bowed their heads to the dust and given place to the stately stores and residences of our merchants and business men.

Game of all kinds abounded in great profusion in the valley, and the crack of the sportsman's rifle was heard where now are our most populous streets. What was in 1820 designated as a place which would cause "an owl to weep" when flying over its broad territory, has now become a large prosperous city, whose name is known the length and breadth of the land.

A Syracusan can now be found in every corner of the earth, and the exclamation, "I hail from Syracuse," is almost as common as "there goes a Yankee." "Syracuse Salt," and "Syracuse Isms" are spoken of in every place in the Union.

The family of John Savage was the first Irish family that located in Syracuse. Mr. Savage was the father of Richard Savage, Esq., of this city. He was a jovial whole-souled man, and a general favorite in the village.

The only colored family residing in Syracuse in 1824, was the family of Isaac Wales. "Uncle Ike" came to Manlius from Maryland as a slave of the Fleming family, about the year 1810. He worked on the canal while it was being dug, and soon accumulated enough money to purchase his freedom. Eighty dollars was the stipend and price which he paid for himself. He married soon after obtaining his liberty, and settled in this place, which has ever since been his home.

Andrew Fesenmyer was the first German that located in Syracuse.

Captain Jonathan Thayer came here in 1824. He was a very useful and humane man, and in nursing the sick of the village he was always ready and willing to grant his services. In 1832, when the cholera prevailed here to such an alarming extent, he overtaxed his constitution in taking care of Elder Gilbert, pastor of the First Baptist Church, and others. The last person he laid out was Dr. Day. He performed this melancholy duty at 12 o'clock at noon, and before midnight he had gone to his final resting place, mourned by all who knew him.

On the 1st of March, 1809, an act passed the Legislature, creating the town of Salina. On the 20th of March, 1809, the first town meeting under this act was held at the house of Cornelius

Schouten, in Salina village, and the following named persons were elected town officers for one year:

Supervisor, Elisha Alvord; Town Clerk, Fisher Curtis; Assessors, Rufus Danforth, Martin Wandell, Richard C. Johnson and Henry Bogardus; Overseers of the Poor, Martin Wandell and Michael Mead; Commissioners of Highway, Michael Mead, William Bulkley, Jr., and Jonathan Fay; Constables, George Loomis and John Sebring; Collector, John Sebring; Overseers of Highways, John J. Mang, Joseph Marll, Elby Palby, Isaac Averill and Ephraim Clark.

A series of resolutions, creating a pound, and fines on stray cattle, hogs and horses, were passed; also one instructing the Supervisors to raise $100 for the support of the poor.

The following is a copy of the minutes of the Town Meeting, held in the town of Salina in April, 1824.

"At the annual town meeting of the Town of Salina, held at the school house in the village of Salina, April 6th, 1824, the following persons were elected officers in and for said town during the ensuing year:

"Supervisor, Henry C. Rossiter; Town Clerk, James Shankland; Assessors, Henry Lake, J. P. Hicks, A. P. Granger and Michael Mead; Overseers of the Poor, James Harris and Jonathan Stickney; Commissioners of Highways, Ashbel Kellogg, Ruel Case and Asa Phillips; Commissioners of Gospel and School Lots, Thomas McCarthy and James Keith; Commissioners of Common Schools, Henry Lake, Henry Case and Fisher Curtis; Inspectors of Common Schools, Libbeus Gilbert, Barent Filkins, John Wilkinson and Ebenezer Fowler; Collector, Jacob Burgess; Constable at Liverpool, James Calley; Constable at Geddes, James H. Luther; Constable at Syracuse, John B. Creed; Constable at Salina, Samuel R. Matthews and Jacob Burgess; Overseers of Highways, first district, Henry Case; second district, Constant Luther; third district, Fisher Curtis; fourth district, Andrew Wilson; fifth district, Jesse Somington; sixth district, Amos P. Granger; seventh district, Rowland Stafford; eighth district, Erastus Perkins; Jesse Somington, pound master, Liverpool; James H. Fuller, pound master, Geddes; J.W. Woodward's yard, public pound; Joshua Forman, public pound, Syracuse; Henry Young, hog-pen, public pound.

"A vote was taken that Path Masters be Fence Viewers.

"Voted that $300 be raised for the support of the poor

"Voted that $200 be raised for the building and repairing of bridges in said town.

"Voted that all town officers be chosen by ballot (except constables) and be chosen by a general ticket.

"Voted to petition the next Legislature for a privilege to dispose of the gospel and school lots in said town.

"Voted to adjourn this meeting to the first Tuesday in April, 1825, as this place.

J. SHANKLAND, Clerk."

Syracuse then formed part of the town of Salina, and was not incorporated as a village until the winter of 1824-25. Up to that time Syracuse flourished under town laws, together with such rules and regulations as were from time to time adopted by mutual consent, and acknowledged as the established regulations of the embryo city.

At a meeting of the freeholders and inhabitants of the village of Syracuse, held pursuant to notice at the school house in said village, on Tuesday, the 3d day of May, 1825, the following officers were chosen and proceedings had:

Trustees, Joshua Forman, Amos P. Granger, Moses D. Burnett, Heman Walbridge and John Rogers; Clerk, John Wilkinson; Treasurer, John Durnford; Pound Master, Henry Young; Constables, Jesse D. Rose and Henry W. Durnford; Overseers of Highways, first district, Henry Young; second district, John Garrison.

I certify the above to be a true statement of the proceedings of the meeting, and that the officers above named were duly elected in pursuance of the act to incorporate the village of Syracuse.

DANIEL GILBERT,
Justice of the Peace, Presiding
Syracuse, May 3d, 1825.

I stated in a former chapter of the *Reminiscences of Syracuse* that Frederick Horner was the only man now living in this city who had ever seen General Washington.

In casting my eye over the city at that time I did not think of the venerable Major Forman, although I had frequently conversed with him about Washington, his dress and personal appearance, and also about the Evacuation of New York by the British army.

Meeting him a few days since I requested him to give the circumstances of the Evacuation, of which Major Forman was an eye-witness, and also his recollections of Washington.

The following is the old gentleman's reply:

Syracuse, Jan'y 30th, 1857

Timothy C. Cheney, Esq:

Dear Sir--Yesterday you observed to me, that you heard that I had seen General Washington, and asked if I would relate to you some common or prominent occurrences of his life, since the Revolution.

When the British troops evacuated the city of New York I lived there, but was very young: it was a great day. I strolled away up to the Bowery lane, 'till I met the British and American armies on a stand, the British in front, the American perhaps one hundred feet in the rear. The general officers of the two armies withdrawn in order to adjust the etiquette of movements to be observed. When I passed the British I hurried on the sidewalk for fear of them. When I arrived at the open space I pounced in between the two armies, and felt secure by the blue coats. Presently an officer stept up and took hold of one of my hands and observed, "Don't be afraid, Sammy; I know you and your brother, Colonel Jonathan. We have belonged to the same division. My name is Colonel Cummins." I then remembered him. He held my hand until the order was given, "Forward, March," when the Colonel told me to go on the side walk, and keep there or I might be run over.

The British army retreated, and the Americans advanced. Between the stand and Wall street the British wheeled off to the left and embarked on board of their fleet in the East river. The Americans kept down Queen (now Pearl) street, and on to Fort George on the Battery. Now came a dead stand, the enemy had greased the flagstaff so that no man could climb it. After many trials a little boy about 12 or 13 years of age came forward and said he could climb it. He had a sailor's frock and trousers, perhaps tarred and sanded. The little fellow fastened the halyards about himself and performed the noble act. Up went the Stars and

Stripes banner, triumphantly fanning the Eagle, while he picks the blinded eyes of the Lion, and the shouts of the Washingtonians reached sky high. Many hats were circulated among the crowd, in favor of the intrepid youth; but whether the young hero was the true receiver of it is a question that never can be answered. It is a strong reflection upon Congress that a suitable donation never has been made.

It is not out of place here to mention the manner of General Washington's taking leave of the officers in service on that day. I don't know it, only on good authority. He requested his officers to meet him at 12 o'clock M. at Sam Francis' Hotel in New York, to take leave of each other. At the appointed time, when all were assembled, the General requested the officers to come up to him to take leave. General Knox, being the highest in rank, advanced. General Washington rose; they embraced each other most affectionately, without uttering a word.   Each according to rank (probably) then advanced.   The scene must have been most interesting. When this affecting business was done, the General left the room, and they accompanied him to Whitehall wharf, where was a barge elegantly equipped, manned by sea captains, in white frocks, to row him to Elizabethtown Point or Powleshook, to take the stage, on his way to where Congress was sitting. In the crowd and hurly burly of the day, I did not get sight of the General. My brother-in-law, Major Ledyard, urged me to go with him, and be introduced to the General, when he was first President, and when Congress sat in New York, but I then declined the opportunity like a foolish boy.

The first time that I saw the General was when the Convention met in Philadelphia, to form the Constitution. He was dressed in citizen's dress, blue coat, his under dress I don't remember; cocked hats were then in fashion, long hair in que and craped and powdered. He most always walked alone, and seemed borne down in thought. The Convention was held in the State-house.   When he came opposite he crossed straight over; he seemed not to wish to speak as he passed. When he stopped upon the steps a plain looking man (perhaps a non-commissioned officer) most profoundly bowed to him. The General noticed him and returned the salute by touching his hat, but made no stop. He presided over the Convention. A little previous to the General's appearance the venerable and much respected Doctor Franklin, a member of the Convention, was brought by men in his sedan and set down in the hall of the State House; the careful men opened the door of the sedan and helped him out, but he was so much afflicted with the palsy that he could not raise his feet, but shuffled them on the floor, and went into the Convention room.

The winter of 1792-93, I spent in Philadelphia, until some time in March. The 4th of March, 1793, was the commencement of the second term of the President of the United States. General George Washington was unanimously re-elected. The large room in the State House was fixed for the accommodation of spectators, in amphitheater fashion.

The day was pleasant. A few steps within the doors of this room and the adjoining three handsome chairs were placed at the foot of the great seats just mentioned; the house was crowded to appearance, so that another person could not crowd in. Precisely at 12 o'clock, the word he's come rang through the house. His coach and one pair drove up to the door. A few persons tried to persuade him to go with four horses and a military guard of honor, but the proposal was condemned. The President walked through the crowd as easy as if the floors were empty; the people opened, and as the President passed, the passage was filled up. It reminded me of a boat passing through water opening and filling up the space. The President took his chair, the center of the three, Chief Justice Cushing on his right, and Senator ---of New Hampshire on his left, the Vice President having left Congress for home.

After a few moments of profound silence, the Senator (a most elegant person), rose from his seat and stept directly before the President, and courteously addressed him, "Are you, Sir, ready to take the oath of office, as President of the United States of North America?"

The President had a small paper in his left hand, I think. He replied in the affirmative. Some words passed which I did not hear. Chief Justice Cushing then rose up, with a large Bible opened through the center. The President placed his right hand (I believe) on the book. The Judge began by saying, "I, George Washington," and he repeated after the Judge.

After the oath was administered they took their seats a few minutes. The President rose, with his hat in his hand, he faced towards the ladies, made his conge, bowing to the right, to the center, and to the left, and one graceful bow to the multitude. All this was performed with a degree of solemnity that I never saw surpassed on leaving church.

A short time previous to this Major Washington, a nephew of the General, died. The President was dressed in deep mourning, his elegant long sword with crepe on the hilt, black shoe and knew buckles (pantaloons were not worn then), his hair craped and powdered, tied behind in a silk bag with black ribands.

When he rose to take the oath of office his position was truly graceful and easy, his right arm extended, his left hand holding his sword by his thigh, point downwards. His shoe buckles covered much of his feet. At that time knee and stock buckles were worn. Often they were costly articles, made sometimes of gold or silver, and set with costly stones. No moustaches or whiskers were worn by Americans, but always neatly shaved, powdered and long ques down the back, or braided, or clubbed. Ruffles over the hand and in the bosoms of the shirts, and an elegant gold or silver brooch.

I was very fortunate in getting a stand against one side of the great door between the rooms, and within ten feet of the President, and a view of all the spectators. The theater like seats prepared for the ladies gave them a full view; it formed a half circle. Every eye seemed to be fixed on Washington.

I have understood that General Washington was an elegant minuet dancer, though he very seldom performed. I lately saw in a paper that when his headquarters were at Newburgh that he performed with a Miss Wynkoop, or another lady, I forget which.

I hope that this rough sketch will be of some little satisfaction to you.

Your friend,
S.S. FORMAN

Major Forman did not tell me his age, but he is a venerable man. His brothers were officers in the American army during the Revolution. They were stationed in New Jersey and were engaged in the battle of Monmouth and several other engagements fought in that state.

Major Forman is a man of wealth, and has filled several public offices in this state with honesty and ability, and has always borne an unblemished character throughout a long and useful life. He is one of the last of that indomitable race of men who lived during the Revolution, and no history has yet recorded the names of their equals.

SALINA

I have been kindly furnished by Mrs. John O'Blennis of Salina with the following facts in regard to the early settlement of that portion of our city.

Mrs. O'Blennis is now over seventy years of age, and her memory in regard to the early settlement of Salina is as perfect as though the occurrences which she relates had taken place within a year. She was the daughter of Isaac Van Vleck, one of the first settlers in Salina.

Mr. Van Vleck moved to Salina from New Galway, in Saratoga county, with a family of four children. He arrived in Salina on the 2d day of March, 1792. Mr. Van Vleck's family was the sixth family that settled in Salina.

A Mr. Whitcomb came to Salina with Mr. Van Vleck. They found at Salina a Mr. Hopkins, engaged in the manufacture of salt in what were then called "salt works."

These salt works consisted of an eight or ten pail kettle hung to different poles, each end of the pole being placed in the crotch of a post set in the ground, and a fire built under the kettles between a few stones which were laid up on each side to condense the heat, and no improvement has been made on that mode since that time.

The salt manufactured at that time was of a greyish color. This color was produced by boiling the bitterns in and mixing them with pure salt. The art of separating the impurities of the salt was discovered by a Mr. Dexter, a blacksmith, two or three years after that date.

John Danforth, a brother to General Asa Danforth, lived in Salina in 1792, and was engaged in the manufacture of salt. He being one of the few fortunate enough to own a kettle large enough to make salt in. He sold the salt for fifty cents per bushel at the works.

Pharis Gould, father of Pharis Gould of this county, lived in Salina in 1792. He was also a salt manufacturer.

A surveyor by the name of Josiah Olcott was a resident of Salina at the time. He was engaged in laying off and surveying the roads in and about the county, and laying out the street of the village then in embryo. When not surveying he was employed as an advisor and middle man about the salt works.

There was a man by the name of Sturge, with his family then living in Salina. Mr. James Peat and several others came that year.

These early settlers were all attracted there by, and had something to do with, the manufacture of salt. They lived very highly on game and fish, of which there was a great supply. The Onondaga Lake and Creek were filled with as fine salmon and other varieties of fish as were ever eaten by any people. The inhabitants were supplied with fish and game by the Indians in great abundance.

There were no clearing in or around the village except here and there a place where nature had refused to do its work of rearing lofty trees, and had left a small , prairie-like spot of green. These places the emigrants had took to cultivate and settle upon.

There was such an open space near the salt spring, a little south of the pump house. There were also several such open spots on each side of Onondaga Creek, that were occupied by the Onondaga Indians; they having built small brush and bark huts, which they used while fishing and hunting , but not as permanent residences. Their permanent places of abode was where the present Indian castle and village now stand.

There were a great many Indians belonging to this tribe living at that time. They were continually roving in all directions seeking game, watching their enemies. At that time there was not a very good existing between our people and the inhabitants of Canada and the frontier. The Indians had a perfect knowledge of all that transpired on the frontier. This knowledge they communicated from tribe to tribe by means of runners. They had a perfect and systematic arrangement of this human telegraph, by means of which they communicated with each other from Albany to Buffalo with the greatest precision and dispatch.

The head chief, Kiactdote, was one of the most cautious and observing men that ever ruled this tribe. He had perfect command of, and exerted a great influence over them. To illustrate his power I must relate an incidence which took place in 1793.

At Green Point, on one of the small prairies, a Mr. Lamb had settled with his family. He had a daughter about 14 years old, who was left in his rude house alone while he attended his agricultural pursuits. Mr. Lamb heard a noise in the house, and going there saw a young Indian kissing his daughter and taking other improper liberties with her. He was so enraged that he picked up a junk bottle belonging to the Indian, and struck the savage on the head, killing him on the spot. He then fled to the settlement of Salina for safety.

The Indians in the vicinity declared they must have the life of Mr. Lamb, according to their custom of "life for a life." The people called the chiefs together and with Webster as their interpreter, related the circumstances as they transpired. Upon receiving this information a council of the tribe was called at Salina. (It was the last council ever held there.) When the council had assembled, Kiactdote stepped into the ring formed by the Indians, threw off his blanket, gave three whoops, making a motion with both hands at the same time. The meaning of this performance was, "pay attention to what I say." He then related the whole circumstances to the nation, and said that it was the first time an Indian had ever been known to insult a white squaw. Although they had many, many prisoners of white blood, no Indian had ever been found so low as to degrade himself and the tribe by insulting a white squaw until this occurrence. That the killing was justifiable, and that Mr. Lamb must not be punished. His decision was acquiesced in and adopted by the tribe, with the proviso that Mr. Lamb should pay to the relatives of the Indian killed a three-year old heifer, which was to cement peace and good will between the posterity of both parties forever. The Indian was buried on the spot where he was killed.

At that time the whites used to require the children to drive their cows one mile from the settlement and watch over them during the day, for fear of being surprised by the enemy from Canada.

In 1793 the ill will between the inhabitants of New York and Canada had risen to such a point that it was deemed necessary for the security and protection of the inhabitants in and around Salina to erect a Block House. The State caused an immediate survey to be made, and the location for the Block House determined upon. A spot of ground immediately in front of the Salina Pump House, near where the canal runs was selected for the proposed site.

The building was finished before 1795. It was 20 feet in height, with port holes arranged in each story to fire from, in case of necessity. The block house was used as a defense against the occasional incursions of guerilla parties from Canada, which the inhabitants feared more that the Indians.

Among the persons present when the block house site was selected was Baron Steuben. Moses DeWitt of Pompey, Isaac VanVleck, William Gilchrist, Gen. Asa Danforth, Mr. Olcott of Pompey and Aaron Bellows. Baron Steuben and Moses DeWitt took supper and lodged at Mrs. O'Blennis's father's house. The Baron was a large and corpulent man, pleasing in his address and manners.

Rev. Mr. Sickles, an itinerant minister used to stop at Mr. Van Vleck's on his way through the country, to an from the frontier. Mr. Van Vleck's house was a common stopping place for most travelers through the country. He did not keep tavern, but he afforded rest to the weary and food to the hungry.

At that time the inhabitants of Salina did not have any wells. The water they used for drinking and cooking was brought from a fresh water spring under the hill near what was then the marsh.

The lake at that time was five or six feet higher than at the present day, and covered the flats at certain seasons of the year.

In 1792, Mr. Gould built what was called a mud house. It was similar to a stick chimney, narrow strips of boards being laid flatways about half an inch apart, and the open spaces filled with mud. The roof was made with split logs running lengthwise from the peak to the eaves.

The first frame house was built by Gen. Danforth and Mr. Van Vleck in 1793. The lumber, or most of it, was brought from Little Falls and Tioga Point in bateaux. The nails came from Albany. That year Thomas Orman, Simon Pharis and William Gilchrist came to Salina. Mr. Orman brought the first cauldron kettle for the manufacture of salt. Mr. Aaron Bellows came that year and established a cooper shop for the manufacture of salt barrels.

Mr. Van Vleck went to Albany that year and brought a large copper mill and placed it in Mr. Bellow's cooper shop, which all families used to grind their corn with. This was an improvement upon the scalloped stump and sweep.

There were no grist or saw mills in this section of the country at that time. There was a small saw mill at Jamesville, but it was not accessible from Salina, as there were no roads for the passage of teams.

Benjamin Carpenter kept the first store in Salina. He kept a large variety store, and traded in furs, salt, etc. with the Indians and settlers. He commenced business in 1795.

In 1794, Patrick Riley, Mr. Thompson, and several others came to Salina to live. The village at that time had increased to thirty-three persons, and of this number thirty were sick: only three being able to attend to their sick neighbors, which they did with the assistance of the Indians.

In 1794 Elisha Alvord, than a young man, in company with several others, came to Salina to reside. Mr. Alvord was elected the Supervisor of the town of Salina at its first town election. He was the father of Thomas and Cornelius Alvord, now residents of Salina.

In 1794, Judge Richard Sanger, Mr. Andrews, of New Hartford, Thomas Hart, of Clinton, Oneida Co., Butler, of Pompey, Mr. Keeler of Onondaga, Asa Danforth, of Onondaga Hollow, and Elisha Alford, of Salina, formed a company called the "Federal Company," for the purpose of manufacturing salt. They put up some of the first six kettle blocks. The company failed in 1801 by inexperience in the business. They had wood merely by cutting it, and salt sold readily at high prices.

Dioclesian Alvord came here in 1796, and hired part of the "Federal Works" with four kettles. He added two more, and with his six kettles he could manufacture eighteen to twenty bushels of salt per day, which he readily sold for 50 cents per bushel.

The pump house was then out in the water and Mr. Alvord had to take a skiff to reach it. The water was pumped by hand and conveyed in troughs to the reservoir made of hollow logs.

The first law suit tried in Salina was the suit of Dr. Barber against John Lamb. The suit was in regard to alleged overcharges on the part of the Doctor, and was tried before Squire Kinne, of Manlius, who came there to accommodate the parties.

Doct. Barber was one of the first physicians in the village of Salina, and son-in-law of John Danforth, of that place.

In 1792 there were about six log and two mud houses in Salina. Three of these houses stood on Salina street, and two or three stood on the spot where Widow Miller now lives. These were built together, or adjoining each other, with separate entrances.

Village lots were not in market in '92, and when a person wanted to build he took such a location as suited him, and put up his house. When the lots came into market, the person building got a pre-emption title for forty dollars.

In 1795 Judge Stevens, the first salt Superintendent, William Gilchrist and Isaac Van Vleck, of Salina, conceived the idea of laying duties on salt. It was thought that the "duties" were not so much for the profit of the State as for the advancement of the personal interests of different parties in Salina.

The idea originated by these men, has been a source of great profit to the State, the State having received prior to 1843 in duties upon salt, over $3,000,000.

The first duties on salt were four pence per bushel. Upon the opening of the canal the duty was raised to one shilling per bushel. The duty is now one cent.

In 1801 Judge Stevens had collected a considerable amount of monies for duties, and was on the point of proceeding to Albany to make a deposit, when he was prevented by sickness and death.

In 1795 the State purchased of the Onondagas the salt lake now called Onondaga lake, with a strip of land one mile in width extending entirely round it, with the exclusive right to all the salt springs, for $500, and the annual payment of one hundred bushels of salt.

The State has from time to time sold to different individuals all the land thus purchased, with the exception of five hundred and forty-nine acres, for which, prior to 1843, they had received in the aggregate, $58,428.25.

The early inhabitants of Salina were a tough, hardy race of men, and withal they were intelligent, energetic and enterprising. They were governed solely by the common law until 1809, when the first town election was held in the town of Salina.

The village increased gradually, and the salt kettles kept pace with the increase of the inhabitants, until now "Salt Point" and "Salt Pointers," and "salt kettles" are known all over the habitable globe.

In 1824 the village of Salina was about one-third as large as at the present day, and its inhabitants were known as the most intelligent, enterprising set of men. It grew rapidly during that year.

The first tax levied upon the inhabitants after the incorporation of the village of Syracuse, was in the fall of 1825. It amounted to $250, a striking contrast to the sum now levied upon the city of Syracuse for municipal purposes. Henry W. Durnford was the collector, and John Durnford was his bail.

In the year 1802, Judge Oliver R. Strong came from Berkshire, Mass., to the county of Onondaga, and located at Onondaga Hill. He was among the first of the settlers who acted in an official capacity, having been appointed a Deputy Sheriff in 1803, by Elijah Rust. This office was held for several years. In 1808 he was appointed County Treasurer by the Board of Supervisors, and served in that capacity for the extraordinary period of 22 years. He has been one of the judges of the county, and President of the Onondaga County Bank, for a long period. In all the relations of life he has borne a reputation for integrity second to no man in the community.

In 1803, Judge Strong, in connection with Cornelius Longstreet, acted as clerk of the election. At that time the elections continued for three days, and the polls were held half a day in a place. The town of Onondaga at that time embraced a large extent of territory, and it was no light duty to act in the capacity of an inspector or clerk of the elections. The responsibility, too, was much greater than at the present time, as the ballot boxes had to be strictly guarded over nights.

In 1802, the village of Onondaga Hill consisted of four framed buildings-two of them erected this year-seven or eight log dwellings or huts, and two log taverns. One of these taverns was kept by Daniel Early, the grandfather of Jonas Early, former canal commissioner. His house stood on the site of the office subsequently occupied by Nehemiah H. Earll, and which still remains on the original lot. The other public house stood about where the store of Mr. Eastman now stands, and was kept by William Lard. Mr. L. was a man of energy and enterprise, and many of his descendants still reside in the county. One of the log huts was used as a blacksmith's shop.

A store was kept by Walter Morgan, but did not have much business.

Medad Curtis was the only lawyer in the place. He was a man of ability, and intelligent and trustworthy; and enjoyed the unbounded confidence of his neighbors. His practice was lucrative.

Two physicians-Doctors Thayer and Colton-were in practice in 1802. They did a large and profitable business, as the inhabitants, like those of all newly-settled countries, were subject to diseases of a bilious character. Few persons were proof against these insidious diseases.

At the time referred to, this county was settling with great rapidity. Many of the settlers were revolutionary soldiers who received their land for services rendered their country in the stirring and eventful contest with Great Britain, and came here to enjoy the blessings of peace and independence which had been acquired by their courage and patriotism.

In 1798-9, Onondaga county was set off from Herkimer, by act of the Legislature. It included the whole of Oswego, and parts of Cayuga and Cortland counties. The territory was divided into eight townships. Soon afterwards a company of gentlemen, consisting of Judge Stevens, Elisha Lewis, Comfort Tyler, John Ellis, Parley Howlett, Sen., Asa Danforth, Thaddeus M. Wood, Elijah Rust, William Lard, Medad Curtis, and Geo. Hall, conceived the idea of making a large village at or near the centre of the county. After a full view of the merits of the different localities, they selected Onondaga Hill, by reason of its high and airy location. The valleys were avoided, because they were regarded as very unhealthy. This company purchased parts of farm lots 104 & 119, and employed Judge Geddes to lay them out into village lots, with a suitable site in the centre for a court house and jail. The plan was faithfully carried out, and these buildings, erected soon afterwards, were placed on the spot thus indicated. The site was very capacious, consisting of fifteen acres, with a gentle declivity towards the north, bounded on every side by public streets.

A few years only elapsed before it became apparent that this attempt at a speculation must fail. The "Hollow" improved faster than the "Hill", and the Erie canal eventually killed both. But it is not the only instance illustrating the want of foresight in the shrewdest men. Comfort Tyler, Thaddeus M. Wood, Gen. Danforth, and their associates in this enterprise, were men far more sagacious than the generality of our pioneer citizens, but they were not aware of the fact that the marts of commerce, trade and wealth, are always found in valleys, and not on mountain elevations.

The people of Onondaga Valley have been their own worst enemies. They not only made no effort to secure the location of the court house, but actually prevented the laying out of the Erie canal through their village, by placing obstacles in the way of Judge Forman, who was sincerely desirous of running that great artery of trade and prosperity through the place. Had the leading property holders exhibited the spirit of a true liberality, the canal would have been carried up to that point from Lodi, and down on the west side of the valley. Thus does selfishness generally defeat its own aims and purposes.--Had the canal taken this direction, Onondaga Valley would have occupied the position now maintained by the City of Syracuse.

The first court held in this county was in the corn house of Comfort Tyler, nearly opposite the late residence of Gen. T. M. Wood (now the residence of Morris Pratt), at Onondaga Valley. After this they were held for some time in the parlor of Mr. Tyler's public house, and subsequently in other public places in different parts of the town, to suit the convenience of the litigants.

At that time there was no jail in the county and the authorities were compelled to take the prisoners to the Herkimer county jail for confinement.

In the year 1804 the county of Oneida had completed a jail in the town of Whitesboro, to which the criminals of this county were transferred-the Legislature having previously passed an act granting this county the right to use the nearest jail. The Whitesboro jail was used until 1810; that year our jail was finished.

In 1801, the Board of Supervisors, then composed of the wisest men in their respective towns, began to take measures to build a court house and jail for this county. Three commissioners - Messrs. Elisha Lewis, Medad Curtiss, and T.M. Wood - were selected to superintend their erection, and by a vote it was determined to locate them on Onondaga Hill. The commissioners did not seem to have much system about building. The buildings were erected by piecemeal and by different persons. The commissioners commenced by contracting with William Bostwick, of Auburn, to put up the frame and enclose the house. This was done in 1802, and closed Mr. Bostwick's contract. Previous to raising the house the people of the Hill collected together and made a "bee" for the purpose of cutting away the trees to make room for the new building. The square was at that time covered with a heavy growth of timber. In order to have the use of the court house, a temporary floor and seats were put into it, and the courts held there till the commencement of 1804. The county then began to feel able to finish the court room and jailor's dwelling. The commissioners contracted with Mr. Abel House to do the carpenter work inside, leaving out the cells; and with a Mr. Sexton, from New Hartford to do the mason work; and Mr. E. Webster to furnish the brick for chimneys. The court room and dwelling were completed during that season. After a year or two preparations were commenced for building the cells of the jail. A contract was made with Roswell and Sylvenus Tousley, of Manlius, to do the iron work for a stipulated price of two shillings per pound. I am not informed who did the wood work, but the cells were not finished till the year 1810.

This jail was a wooden building, 50 feet square, two stories high, with a square roof pitching four ways to the eaves. It was not painted. This finishing touch was done by a subscription some years afterwards, by the people of Onondaga Hill. The first story was appropriated for the jail and the dwelling of the janitor, a hall separating them from each other. The cells were constructed of heavy oak plank, fastened together with wrought spikes. The doors were made of a like material, with a "diamond" in the center to pass through the food and give light to the prisoners. In the rear of the cells were grated windows. The court room was reached by a stairway leading from this hall. The judges' bench was directly in front of the entrance to the court room and was constructed in a circular form. The whole cost of the building was $10,000 - a large sum, apparently for such a structure; but when it is considered that the work was done mostly on credit, there will be no occasion for surprise. Besides the system of keeping public account at that day was very imperfect. Many of the bills contracted in the erection of the building were not paid until several years afterward.

This court house and jail were used for the purpose designed until the year 1829. The first jailor was James Beebee, a Revolutionary soldier, and father of Mrs. Victor Birdseye of Pompey. His successor was Mason Butts, father of Horace Butts, who was jailor after the removal of the county buildings to Syracuse. John H. Johnson, Esq., also acted as jailor there for several years.

Syracuse having in 1825-26, grown to be the largest town in the county, the propriety of removing the county buildings to that place began to be agitated. The people on the Hill strongly resisted the measure, and in the first mentioned year succeeded in getting a bill through the legislature, providing for their retention of that place; but through the influence of the Syracuse Company, Gov. Clinton was induced to veto it, and it was thus defeated. But the project did not sleep. In 1827-28, a law was enacted authorizing the Supervisors of the county to erect a court house and jail within the corporate limits of the village of Syracuse. In obedience to the requirement of this act, the Supervisors, in the summer of 1828 met in the village of Syracuse, at the public house kept by James Mann (now the Syracuse House), to take into consideration the selection of a site for the proposed buildings, and also to make the necessary preparations for erecting the same. At that meeting there was a great deal of discussion upon the question, and a wide difference of opinion existed among the members relative to the site of the buildings. On taking a vote it resulted in placing it midway between Syracuse and Salina, in consideration of the village of Salina presenting to the county a full and unencumbered title to the property, consisting of not less than three acres and $1000.

As an inducement to locate it in the center of the village, Messrs. Townsend & James offered the county, free of expense, all that block of land on which the Onondaga County and Syracuse Bank are now located, with the exception of one lot on which the First Presbyterian Church then stood on the corner of Salina and Fayette streets. This offer was refused, but as the sequel proved, it would have been much the best bargain, for this property is now worth at least ten times as much as the court house lot was recently sold for, besides being a much more convenient site for county buildings. But the site having been fixed, could not be changed.

At this meeting measures were also taken for the erection of the county buildings by the appointment of three men, styled building commissioners, consisting of John Smith, Thomas Starr, and Samuel Forman, with power to cause plans and specifications to be made, and to contract for the erection of buildings. The County Treasurer was also empowered to borrow $20,000 in two annual installments of $10,000 each. After the plans were submitted, the commissioners decided to build the jail of stone, fifty feet square, and two stories high, with a hall and stairs in the center.

The south half was designed for the jailor's dwelling, and the north half for strong stone cells and the second story over the cells was appropriated for cells for debtors, witnesses, etc. The court house was to be built of brick, sixty feet square with large columns on the west side, and two stories high. The first story was divided by a hall into four apartments, in each corner, for the use of the grand and petit juries, and other purposes. The court room occupied all of the second story except the landing of the stairs and two petit jury rooms in each corner. The Judges' seat was in the south side, opposite the landing of the stairway.

These were the county buildings the commissioners decided upon and invited bids for their erection. In the spring of 1829 the bids were received according to the specifications and plans. Mr. John Wall obtained the contract for the building of the jail, which was erected by him in early 1829. The cells in this jail were of the strongest kind. Since it was taken down they have been placed in the basement of the new courthouse on Clinton Square.

L. A. Cheney and Samuel Booth obtained the contract for doing the mason work of the court house, and David Stafford obtained the contract for doing the carpenter work. It was put up that year and enclosed. In the following year Mr. Wall made a bargain with the commissioners to complete the edifice, and during that year it was finished, ready for the occupation of the courts.

The estimate for these buildings proved to be some thirty per cent. short of their expense - the total cost of them having been upwards of $27,000.

The jail was abandoned in 1850 after the erection of the Penitentiary, and the removal of the jail prisoners to that institution. The materials were used in the erection of the work-shops at the Penitentiary and the new court house.

Attempts were made from time to time to change the site of this court house, but they all failed until after the destruction of the building by fire on the morning of 5th January 1856.

It was not long after the erection of the court house midway between Syracuse and Salina, before complaints arose in regard to its locality. The expectation which was entertained that business would center about it was not realized; and hence it was not accessible to the public. The inconvenience was, however, partially submitted to for about twenty years before any serious movement was made to change the site. Some five or six years ago, Gen. Granger submitted a proposition to the Board of Supervisors to this effect: that he would build a good court house on any lot in the heart of the city that might be designated in consideration of the conveyance to him of the old Court House site and $20,000 in money. This offer received very little favor at the hands of the Board. During the annual session of the Board in 1853, the subject was again introduced by Hon. Sanford C. Parker, Supervisor from Van Buren, who proposed a resolution that the county should unite with the city in the erection of an edifice of sufficient dimensions for a court house, clerk's office, city hall, etc. Mr. P. made an able speech in support of the policy, but it failed. The matter was then suffered to rest until the session of the Board in Dec. 1855. On the 3rd day of that month, Mr. Midler, Supervisor from DeWitt, offered a resolution of inquiry on the subject, proposing to instruct the Committee on "Court House and Clerk's office," consisting of T.C. Cheney, E. A. Williams, and Joel Fuller, "to examine and report to this Board the expense of building a new court house, and what the premises, where the old one stands, will sell for." The resolution was adopted without objection. The committee, thus instructed, proceeded to discharge the duty imposed upon them and on the 7th of December submitted a report, embodying such facts bearing on the matter as they were enabled to gather. This report, after reciting various reasons for the removal of the court house - among which were that extensive repairs of the old edifice were annually required; that its internal arrangement were inconvenient; that it was a long distance from the centre of trade; that business was consequently delayed and court expenses multiplied, etc. etc. - concluded with a resolution proposing "that a committee of three be appointed whose duty shall be, at some subsequent meeting of this Board, to report a plan for the sale of the present court house premises - to examine and report upon a suitable site or sites for a new court house, and the terms on which title thereto can be secured to the county, and also plans and estimates for a new court house.

This report was laid on the table until the 14th, when it was called up and after a slight modification adopted by a vote of 15 to 9, as follows:

Ayes---Messers. Cooper, Midler, Bailey, Knapp, Fuller, Adams, Salmons, Wells, Patten, Palmer, Greenfield, Hawley, Stevens, Trowbridge, Cheney --15.

Noes---Young, Little, Hamilton, Bishop, Holbrook, Moseley, Mason, Gere, Yorky--9.

On the following day the Chair named the following committee to act under the resolution, to wit: T. C. Cheney, Luke Wells and D. T. Moseley. (Mr. Wells subsequently declined serving, and Mr. Patten, of Salina, was substituted.) On the 16th of January ensuing, Mr. Cheney, from the committee, submitted a majority report, recommending a change of site and the erection of a new court house. Mr. Moseley dissented from the majority, on the ground that the tax-payers of the county were unfavorable to the project. The reports having been submitted, Mr. Little, of Clay, moved to lay the majority report on the table, and the motion prevailed by a vote of 16 to 9, and the report of Mr. Moseley was adopted in lieu thereof, by ayes 15, noes 8.

On the following day the Board, having as they supposed, completed the year's business, adjourned *sine die*, little anticipating that the "Court House Question" would be speedily settled, as event proved. Early in the morning of the 5th of February, our citizens were aroused by the cry of "fire!" The incendiary had been at his nefarious work, and the old court house was found his victim. Within an hour the building was a heap of blackened ruins. There was no longer any question as to the necessity of erecting a new court house. But, of course, nothing could be done without a meeting of the Board of Supervisors. A call was therefore put into circulation, which received the signatures of the majority of the Board and a meeting was got together on the 13th of February. At this meeting a committee, consisting of T.C. Cheney, George Stevens and William F. Gere, were appointed to report at the next meeting of the Board, relative to the location and price of lots that might be offered for sites for a new court house. There was some opposition to any action by that Board, but the majority were favorable to prompt measures.

The Board again met on the 14th of April, when the majority of the committee---Messers. Cheney and Stevens--- reported in favor of changing the court house site, and the erection of a new edifice. Mr. Gere dissented to that portion relating to a change of site, and the Board sustained him on a call of the yeas and nays - by a vote of 14 to 13 - a two-third vote being necessary. But on the following day the Board receded, by adopting a resolution offered by Mr. Chapman of Onondaga, "that is an equal exchange (with Col. Voorhees) of the present court house site, for a lot on Clinton Square, this Board will order the exchange." This proposition was adopted by a vote of 20 to 6, and on motion of Mr. Barrow, T.C. Cheney, Elizur Clark, and Bradley Carey, were appointed a committee "to prepare plans, specifications, and estimates for a court house, and report at a future meeting." The Board then adjourned to the 28th of April, when this committee submitted the following report:

To the Honorable Board of Supervisors:

The special committee, raised at the last meeting of this Board, to consider the subject of exchanging court house sites and preparing plans, specifications and estimates for a new court house, beg leave to report:

That, owing to the absence of Col. Voorhees, for a portion of the time, the committee have been somewhat delayed in the progress of their negotiations with him. They have, however, found no difficulty in arriving at such and understanding for the transfer of sites as they think the Board should approve. The terms of the exchange which he proposes, and which the committee have approved, are the same, substantially, as were contemplated by the resolution under which the committee was selected.

In reference to the plan of the proposed structure, the committee has adopted that of Mr. H. N. White, which was presented to the Board at the last meeting, with some slight modifications. This plan is herewith presented, drawn on a large scale, so as to be clearly comprehended. The estimated expenses of the building on the plan proposes is $28,000, including old material. This estimate includes the placing of cells in the basement and has been made by competent mechanics, and embraces everything with the exception of the furniture necessary for the edifice when completed.

The committee had under consideration the relative cost of brick and stone for the structure; and finding that the expenses of the latter would be no more that eight per cent. in excess of the former, came to the unanimous conclusion to recommend the use of the Onondaga stone. This material is not only the most appropriate for the purpose, but more durable than brick.

If the Boards should adopt this plan the county of Onondaga will soon have a better and more convenient court house than any other county in the State. Nor will any of them have a temple of justice more central, or more commanding in appearance.

The considerations that have prompted the committee in their action are so apparent that it is hardly deemed necessary to advert to them here. The county of Onondaga is broad in territory, large in population, fertile in resources, and noted for its enterprising character. It must continue to advance with rapid pace in population and wealth. Would it be the part of wisdom for such a county to chaffer about the investment of a few thousand dollars in a building of this description? Should cheapness be substituted for durability and adaptation? The committee think not. They think that the county, having secured a favorable site for this building, should erect an edifice not only well suited to its purpose, but one that will remain for generations as a model in style and durability. Such a one the committee propose, in the confident belief that the Board of Supervisors will concur in their recommendation.

All of which is respectfully submitted.

T. C. Cheney
Elizur Clark
Bradley Carey
Committee
Syracuse, April 28, 1856

The question of changing the site was yet undisposed of, and to test the sense of the Board on that point, Mr. Palmer offered a resolution "that the site of the court house for [the] county, be and is hereby changed to the lot (Block 81) on the corner of Clinton square and Clinton alley." This resolution was adopted by a vote of 24 to 1 as follows:

Yeas---Messrs Hay, Sayles, Freeman, Ludington, Hamilton, Harris, Keene, Emerick, Meade, Bishop, Chapman, Pfohl, Slocum, Stevens, Johnson, Carey, Cheney---24.

Nays---Greenfield---1.

The plan of the building, as presented in the committee's report, was then adopted, and Messrs. Slocum, Johns and District Attorney Andrews were directed to execute the papers for the exchange of sites with Col. Voorhees. The next day Timothy C. Cheney, Luke Wells and D. C. Greenfield were appointed a committee to superintend the erection of the building, and Horatio N. White, Architect. At a subsequent meeting of the board in June the proposals for the erection of the building, advertised for by the Commissioners, were opened, and the contract awarded to Messrs. Cheney & Wilcox, at $37,750, the contractors to have the materials of the old court house and jail. Mr. Cheney thereupon resigned his place as commissioner, and Elizur Clark was appointed to fill the vacancy. Portions of the work were afterwards sub-let---the cut stone work to Spaulding & Pollock; the carpenter and joiner work to Coburn & Hurst; and the iron work to Featherly, Draper & Cole. The building is now in process of construction and will be completed on the first day of October next.

In the year 1821, Judge Forman, who then resided in Syracuse, conceived the idea of manufacturing salt by solar evaporation. Mr. Forman with Isaiah Townsend of Albany, went to New Bedford for the purpose of examining works that had previously been erected there. He met in that noted sea-faring town Stephen Smith with whom he counselled upon the subject.

Upon Mr, Formans' statements in regard to the strength of the water, its purity and abundance, Mr. Smith consented to embark in the enterprise of erecting a similar works here. This gentleman together with William Rotch, Jr, Samuel Rodman, and James Arnold, of New Bedford, formed the "Onondaga Salt Company." Of this company, Mr. Smith was the controlling agent, and Henry Gifford superintended the construction.

Subsequently to the formation of this company, Judge Forman proceeded to Albany and procured the passage of a law by the legislature, authorizing the companies to take possession of the grounds and erect the necessary works.

He also endeavored to induce William James, and Isaiah and John Townsend to form another company and embark in the manufacture of coarse salt, but they then declined. He then applied to Henry Eckford, the celebrated naval architect of New York, who consented, and with other gentlemen established "The Syracuse Salt Company." Judge Forman was appointed Agent of this company and Matthew L. Davis, Secretary.

Mr. Eckford was then owner of the "Walton Trace" which he had purchased of Wilson, Sabine and Forman. Before the works of this company had far advanced, William James, Isaiah and John Townsend of Albany, and James McBride of New York, became the proprietors. At that period the Salt Springs were termed the "Old Federal Springs." The water was pumped by hand labor by men perched on high stagings, and collected into rude reservoirs for distribution.

The companies thus formed immediately set about the execution of their plans. The first thing done was to cut away the trees, clear the grounds (the portion between the "Genesee Turnpike" and the Erie Canal was an almost impassable swamp) preparatory to the erection of the vats.

It was essential that a greater supply of water should be procured; accordingly the two companies, at their joint expense, erected the first great reservoir, pumps and aqueducts at Salina; the machinery propelled, as it now is, by surplus water from a branch of the Erie canal. The starting point for the vats was just north of Church street.

After these works were underway, the "Onondaga Salt Company" broke ground west of the creek, near the dwelling subsequently occupied for many years by Joseph Savage. Here the first growth of trees were still standing, and yielded nearly 100 cords of wood to the acre.

The building of vats was prosecuted with great diligence and energy: about two million feet of lumber being consumed annually for several years.

In 1826 Mr. Gifford covered twenty acres of ground on private account, but was unable to procure water for three years. This investment was continued by Mr. Gifford until the land was sold by the State, a year or two since.

Such, in brief was the origin of the coarse salt manufacture. There are now in existence upwards of 23,000 vats or "covers" occupying about 380 acres in which is invested a capital of <u>one million one hundred and sixty-one thousand dollars.</u>

It may not be out of place here to make a brief allusion to Stephen Smith. Mr. Smith in early life was particularly noted for his persevering industry in the pursuit of knowledge. He was the son of Abraham Smith of New Bedford, with whom he learned the trade of a blacksmith, but did not follow the occupation. At the age of twenty-one, he went to New York, found employment in a celebrated commercial firm there and became a partner in a Ship Chandlery establishment, which during his absence in Europe became unsuccessful.

In 1801 he went to England and France on an agency. He made several voyages as Supercargo to India and China. Subsequently he went on different occasions to Italy, Spain and Portugal.

The War of 1812 and ill health detained him at home, and he then embarked in the manufacture of Salts from sea water at Yarmouth on Cape Cod. It was while prosecuting this enterprise that Judge Forman met with and induced him to come to Syracuse, as before stated.

Mr. Smith continued to reside here until his death, which Occurred in 1854. He was a man of strong mind, a close observer of passing events, liberal views, and unbending integrity. No man stood higher in the community that Stephen Smith. The monument at his grave marks the last resting place of "God's noblest work, an honest man."

The first furnace erected west of Oneida County was built by Mr. Nicholas Mickles, father of Phil D., who emigrated from New England to lay the foundation of a fortune in this then frontier country. It is usually called the "old Furnace"and has long been a landmark on the road to Onondaga Hill. Judge Forman was associated in this enterprise with Mr. Mickles, and they did a heavy business for many years in the manufacture of kettles for the western country and the salt works. During the war of 1812 they had a heavy contract with government for supplies of cannon balls and shells. These missiles of death were transported by wagons to Salina, from whence they were taken by water to Oswego and there distributed to various points along the frontier. Mr. Mickles was a man of intelligence and probity, and highly esteemed.

In every community there are men with characteristics so marked as to attract particular notice and comment. Syracuse has not been wanting in this respect. I propose to terminate these random "Reminiscences" by adverting to one of them who was well known to many persons now residing in this vicinity. I allude to James Sackett.

Mr. Sackett originally emigrated from New England and settled in Skaneateles, but removed to Syracuse in 1826, long before which event he acquired the soubriquet of "Old Sackett" by which ever afterwards he was known. He was very eccentric in his habits and conversation. He acquired a large property by the purchase of Land Warrants of revolutionary soldiers and locating the lots in this section of the State. He was very fond of horses of which he raised the finest breed in this country.

In 1824 he contracted with a man to build him a house about 22 feet by 40. It was to be set on his block on Salina street, opposite the Empire. The block was owned by him, and nothing on it except at the south end, where were two or three little buildings. It was a pretty field for a residence. The contractor did not come and put up the house as he had agreed. He then contracted with another builder to put up the same kind of house. It was immediately done. While the second contractor was finishing the first house, the first contractor came with the second house. Although Mr. Sackett was under no obligation to receive the house, he said to the builder: "Here! put it up at the end of this one." Of course he had a house 22 by 80 feet. He had a rough board fence put around the lot, which was entered by a gate swinging on a post in the centre. After his house was finished and he had resided in it a few years, the crickets had taken joint occupancy with him. They were rather noisy, and disturbed the old man. Mr. Sackett was a timid man--so he undertook to expel them. He succeeded very well--with the exception of one old chap that bid him defiance. This fellow was located behind the chimney, where he kept perpetual song. But he was not out of reach of harm. One Monday morning masons were seen at work taking down the chimney, which was razed to the ground, and this noisy old chap driven from his quarters and the chimney rebuilt so as to exclude him thereafter.

Mr. Sackett also had singular tastes in the matter of dress. He wore a frock coat reaching down to his heels, a wide-brimmed hat, with a large veil over his face. Such an outfit on a tall, slim, fleshless man like Mr. Sackett made him an object of notice to every person. He always hired masons to fill his ice house, so that the work would be well done. In doing odd jobs he would hire more men than were necessary, and would often discharge them all before the work on hand was completed. He usually travelled about the country in an old, ricketty buggy, with a patched top of various colors, drawn by a splendid horse. Wherever he went on foot he carried an old umbrella, with a large white patch on top. But with all his oddities he was a well-disposed man, and correct and prompt in business matters. He died worth an estate valued at $150,000.

CONCLUSION AND APOLOGY

It was intended to have continued these Reminiscences down to a later period in the history of the City of Syracuse, but the business season having commenced, the building operations of the author, Mr. Cheney, require his constant attention, and makes this somewhat abrupt suspensions of the Recollections necessary, for the present at least. But we hope to resume them again at some future period and extend the history down to a period within the memory of every inhabitant. In the meantime, we may be pardoned for alluding to the general fidelity to truth, in all the material facts, and even in the minutest detail of these Recollections. A few corrections have been noticed by other old residents of the city, but no material point has been touched, which required any change in the general features of Mr. Cheney's version. Of their interesting character readers can be their own judge.

SOME NOTES ON THE CHENEY REMINISCENCES BY THE REV. W. M. BEAUCHAMP, S.T.D. WITH ADDITIONS FROM OTHERS

In compiling these valuable reminiscences Mr. Johnson sometimes added his own, as in the old mill; and often used his own words, as was proper. Mr. Cheney's notes on Sullivan's expedition are simply what was told him of things happening before his time. They were the distorted tales of frontier life. Sullivan's army never came near here; nor was there any fighting inside the city limits. In the burning of the Onondaga towns by Col. Goose Van Schaick, April '79, the Onondagas fired but once, and this across the creek, harming no one. Later that year however, Col. Gansevoort's party did pass eastward through the county, seeing but one Indian.

The pipe tomahawk came into use but little before the Revolution and this one would probably not antedate 1750. Anteauga (Oundiaga) may have had a medal from Washington, like others, but no historian mentions this and it hardly seem probable. Hostile throughout the Revolution, he opposed white innovations afterward, and died in August 1839, aged 91 years. Kahiktote died in 1808. His name means <u>a thorn tree with fruit upon it.</u>

But few of the Onondagas at first returned. In 1818 there were but 299 here, of all ages, and half that number in 1834. After the sale of the Buffalo Creek reservation, where they had a village, many came back. The location of Nukerck's grave indicates that Webster's camp was not then near the mouth of the creek, but in the heart of the present city. Mr. Cheney's account is of very recent graves ---the Onondaga coming to the valley about 1720.

Few Revolutionary soldiers drew lots on which they lived, these being assigned to New York soldiers only, but these were often sold to veterans from other states. No lots on the Onondaga and Salt Springs reservations were given to soldiers, but many bought them.

Church street is now West Willow; Mulberry is South State; Clinton Alley is Clinton street; Foot is James street; Lodi street connected the villages of Lodi and Salina. Robber's Row laid out in 1825 was a busy street two years later.

The new Roman Catholic Church was St. John's Evangelists, built in 1854 on the corner of Lock and Willow streets. The second St. Paul's church was where the postoffice is yet standing. The last sermon in the first one was delivered April 10, 1842 and the second was consecrated July 5 of the same year.

School House No. 4 is now Genesee School. The old Saleratus factory, corner of Genesee and Clinton streets, was burned August 23, 1859. Mickles furnace was at Elmwood Park on the site of Morris's greenhouse, and Prospect Hill extended from Hickory to Laurel street.

Tioga Point properly is in Athens, PA, but the Indian word is often used where two large streams meet, and the one mentioned with Little Falls is Herkimer, where West Canada Creek enters the Mohawk, receiving the name Te-uge-ga from the Indians.

The first Fourth of July celebration on record here was held in 1820, when Thaddeus M. Wood presided. Samuel M. Hopkins was the orator, and Governor Clinton and other men of note were present. The new canal increased the crowd, the packet boat, Montezuma having come from that place April 21.

When Gurney S. Strong republished these reminiscences in 1894, he omitted some parts and summarized others. The whole pamphlet is given now with but one omission, by request, and summary of the advertisements is added.

In 1857, the date of publication, Clark T. Ames made and sold boots and shoes. C. T. Norton did the same and so did Jacob Balshauzer. Osborn & Hunt supplied groceries and salt meats. Stone & Ball dealt in watches, silverware and jewelry as did Abraham Stern. Colwell & Thurber made jewelry, while George Barney sent fine gold pens throughout the land. L. J. Ormsbee had stationery and Yankee notions. L. Whittemore added book binding and shelf boxes made to order. W. T. Hamilton sold books and wall paper, and so did Peck & Rudd. Dempster Moore kept a drug store as did William B. Tobey. Dr. James Fuller was a consulting chemist and druggist. Dr. B. S. Gay was both a physician and surgeon while Dr. E. B. Lighthills passed as oculist and aurist. R. O. Cossitt's Eagle Saloon furnished lunches, and Olmstead could satisfy hunger. J. O. Bonta sold pipes and tobacco. Charles Carter made planes and other tools. Frederick Humbert supplied furniture and C. Cook made a specialty of mattresses. S. C. Hayden & Co. offered great bargains in both lines. G. M. Barnard was strong on ambrotypes in his photograph gallery but Geer was sure his daguerreotypes were better than any ambrotypes ever made. G. Doris made light carriages. William E. Loftie furnished "invisible ventilating heads of hair." Stoddard & Dawson had a general insurance agency. William Briscoe did whitewashing and hard finishing while Beverly Chase had been an engraver here for fifteen years. Last of all Moses and William Summers appear as publishers of the Standard, the former soon to acquire fame in the Civil War. Of those mentioned by Mr. Cheney, a partial list follows, mostly with dates of death:

The Rev. John W. Adams, D. D. came to Syracuse as pastor of the First Presbyterian Church , June 1826, and died here April 4, 1850 in his 54th year. His twenty-four years' record of members, weddings and baptisms was published by the Genealogical Society of Central New York in 1902, and contains names of many prominent people. He was about to publish a history of Onondaga when J. V. H. Clark bought his material and issued his well-known work.

Zophar H. Adams, general utility man, made Warren street, from Jefferson street to Billings Park.

Dioclesian Alvord died March 10, 1867, aged 73 yrs.

Elisha Alvord, first Supervisor of Salina, died July 1846, aged 73 years.

Thomas Gold Alvord, "Old Salt", came here in June 1826, and died in 1897, aged 87 years. He married Amelia, daughter of Ashbel Kellogg, February 13, 1833. He was long in the New York Assembly and at one time was Lieutenant-Governor.

Hon. Charles Andrews was born in Oneida county May 27, 1827, and became District Attorney in 1853, Judge of the Court of Appeals in 1870, and Chief Justice in 1892. He was also Mayor of Syracuse in 1861-62 and in 1868. He is now Chancellor of the Diocese of Central New York.

Theodore Ashley was in the first fire company and had a furniture shop in 1835 and earlier. In the cholera season of 1832 he had ten funerals one Sunday morning.

Benjamin B. Bacheller was from Roylaston, Mass. and died June 12, 1856 in his 64th year.

Harvey Baldwin, son of Dr. Jonas C. Baldwin, of Baldwinsville, and first Mayor of Syracuse in 1848, died August 22, 1863, aged 67 years. His first wife was Miss Laura Geddes.

The Rev. William Barlow, rector of St. Paul's church, came here in 1827. After leaving here he was recalled but did not come back.

Capt. James Beebee was drowned Sept. 20, 1812, aged 60 years, and was buried at Onondaga Hill. His wife was buried on Pompey Hill.

Aaron Fellows died at Fulton, NY, April 28, 1851, aged 90 years. He was one of the founders of the First Presbyterian Church, Salina, in September 1803. The first services were in his cooper shop.

Dearborn Bickford was afterward a prominent citizen of Manlius village, and innkeeper and postmaster there.

Elijah Bicknall died Aug. 26, 1847, aged 70 years.

Victory Birdseye of Pompey held many important offices, and died Sept. 17, 1853, aged 71 years. He married Capt. James Beebee's daughter.

William K. Blair married Mrs. Celeste Owen, Aug, 29, 1827 and died in 1882 aged 82 years. He built a fine block in Robber's Row.

Henry Bogardus died June 21, 1841, age 71 years, Peter Bogardus, his brother, was another of the Revolutionary soldiers who signed the response for their comrades in 1824. He died April 3, 1836, aged 75 yrs. Both are buried at Orville.

John C. Brown died June 6, 1847, aged 60 years, and was buried at Onondaga Valley.

Major Moses D. Burnet was one of the founders of the First Presbyterian church and the donor of Burnet Park to the city. According to Rev. Mr. Adams he married Miss Helen Creed - not the widow - June 13, 1826. At one time he lived where the century Club has its home. In 1851 he was elected Mayor of Syracuse, and died Dec. 29, 1876 aged 84 years.

Burr Burton was born at Onondaga Hill, April 23, 1804 and married Laura M. Parkhurst, Oct. 29, 1829. He became a salt manufacturer and alderman, dying May 4, 1865 aged 61 years.

Ebenezer Butler, Jr. was born in Connecticut, 1761, was the first settler of Pompey Hill, lived a while in Manlius and died in Ohio Sept. 1829, where he left descendants by his second wife.

Horace Butts died May 9, 1849 aged 48 years. He was assessor and trustee. Mason Butts, his father, died in Onondaga in 1814.

Stephen Cadwell was village president in 1829 and died Feb. 24, 1881 in his 93rd year.

Bradley Carey died Jan. 29, 1893 in his 89th year. He married Matilda Phelps and was village trustee in 1845.

Henry Case has two wives buried in Liverpool cemetery, but there is no stone for him.

Deacon H. Chamberlain died June 5, 1747, aged 61 years.

Abner Chapman, born in Conn., April 30, 1798, died at South Onondaga, June 18, 1873. He married Eliza Merrick in 1821 and Mary Everingham in 1873, and held several public offices.

Lucius H. Cheney was village trustee, 1844-45.

Elizur Clark was born in Saybrook, Conn., Oct 5, 1807, and came to Cicero in 1823. He was an alderman in Syracuse in 1848 and died there Dec. 27, 1895. He married Jerusha Spencer in 1825 and Augusta M. Peck in 1869.

Luke Collins, a famous cattle man of English birth, died Nov. 11, 1893, aged 84 years.

Dr. Walter Colton was at first in Pompey and Manlius. In Pompey he was the first settled physician, and there he married the eldest daughter of Capt. Elizur Brace in the winter of 1796-97. He became Judge of the Court of Common Pleas.

Dr. David S. Colvin died Feb. 2, 1862 in his 77th year. Benjamin Colvin died Dec. 16, 1861, aged 63 years. The Colvins were an influential family, and an early street had its name from them, and still retains it.

Judge George F. Comstock of the Court of Appeals died Sept. 27, 1892 aged 81 years. He took an active part in founding Syracuse University.

Wm. A. Cook, died Nov. 21, 1848, aged 55 years. He was born in Mass., Nov. 7, 1793 and came of Onondaga Hill in 1815, where he married Harriet B. Ellis, Oct. 19, 1816. He was a fine looking man and was brigade-inspector, 1817-36. He was deputy superintendent of salt springs, and also senior warden of St. Paul's church for twelve years.

Sterling Cossitt was landlord of South Salina House, 1815-25, and Syracuse was called Cossitt's Corners.

John P. Creed bought land in Syracuse in 1814, and was elected constable in 1824, probably dying that year.

Elijah W. Curtis was first supervisor of Geddes in 1848, and the first lawyer there. He was also a vestryman of the Apostolic church in Geddes when organized in 1832.

Fisher Curtis died April 27, 1831, aged 51 years and was the first president of Salina village.

Medad Curtis, once influential, had no stone or available record. He was surrogate in 1810. and his widow remarried Dr. Daniels of Salina. She was Mr. Curtis's third wife.

Oris Curtis died Jan. 23, 1801. He was from Farmington, Conn.

Daniel Dana died Dec. 20, 1858, aged 60 years. He erected the Dana Building, or City Boarding House, on West Genesee street.

Gen. Asa Danforth has no stone at his grave, but his name appears in Oakwood on monument of descendants. He died Sept. 2, 1818, one of the most noted men of the region, in his 73rd year. His wife, Hannah Wheeler died in 1837. aged 88 years. In allusion to his dividing his last loaf with a needy neighbor in early days, his obituary notice closed with the following lines on one

"Whose heart was generous, warm and kind,
Whose Lib'ral hand oft clothed and fed
The naked, hungry, halt, and blind,
Or saints or savages might find
and share with Danforth half his bread.
He's gone, and we no more behold
That bounteous hand stretched forth to give.
That hand is stiff - that heart is cold;
So died our patriot sires of old;
Such is the fate of all who live."

Asa Danforth, Jr. was born in Brookfield, Mass, June 29, 1768, is said, in the family history, to have died in Onondaga Valley in Sept. 1818, which was the date of his father's death, erroneously given in the same book as 1837. His residence is usually reported as Salina, His wife, Olive Langdon, died Aug. 29, 1842, aged 75 years. They were married in Jan. 1789. She is buried in Oakwood, but his grave is unknown to me. In Gen. Danforth's will, dated July 4, 1818, Polaski King was made executor, and only Danforth's wife Hannah and son, Adams are mentioned. His other children probably received their portions. The younger Asa and his wife were called a fine looking couple.

John Danforth, Revolutionary soldier, was born in Mass., Feb. 17, 1748, and came to Salina in 1789. The accounts of these early Danforths are somewhat confused and obscure, and the absence of memorial stones is quite remarkable.

Rufus Danforth may have been a son of John, who died in 1813, aged 33 years, and is buried in Liverpool, but he is thought to have been a brother, reported to have been drowned in Oneida Lake.

Benjamin Darling died March 4, 1850, aged 90 years and 2 months, and is buried at Collamer. He was a pensioner and one of the Revolutionary signers of 1824.

Matthew L. Davis, father of Matthew W., was an early merchant and salt manufacturer.

Thomas T. Davis died May 2, 1872, aged 62 years. He was village president in 1841.

Dr. Jonathan Day had a drug store and died of cholera in 1832.

Hiram A. Deming, teacher and bookkeeper, was born in Saratoga county in 1779 and came to Syracuse in 1820. He was village clerk in 1831-32. He bought it is said, a quarter interest in a lottery ticket which drew $50,000.

Pliny Dickinson was a member of the First Presbyterian Church in 1826, and village president ten years later.

Moses DeWitt, early surveyor and great land owner, died Aug. 25, 1794, aged 28 years, and was buried with military honors near Jamesville, where his ruined tomb may be seen.

Rene D. Dillaye, the first of the name here, died Oct. 12, 1847, aged 78 years. Henry A., his son, built stores which were burned in 1855, and rebuilt the next year. He died April 19, 1883, aged 70 years.

John Durnford died May 19, 1867, aged 76 years. He founded the Onondaga Gazette in April 1823 and was long a prominent man.

Henry W. Durnford, police constable in 1825, was in the grocery trade in 1840. In 1842 he was village president, and an alderman in 1848-49. He was buried Sept 4, 1863, aged 70 years.

John Durston d. May 7, 1863 in his 47th year. He had been a teacher.

David Earll died March 29, 1817, in his 87th year.

Jonas Earll died in Oct. 1847 in his 61st year. Jonas Earll, Jr. d. Oct. 28, 1846 in his 61st year. He was elected to Congress in 1826, and the family was influential.

Nehemiah H. Earll died Sept. 1, 1872, age 85. He was elected to Congress in 1838, was Salt Superintendent and held judicial appointments.

Daniel Elliott died April 7, 1843, aged 55 yrs. He was village president in 1830, and father of the artist.

General John Ellis was born in Hebron, Conn., married Submit Olds in 1795, came to Onondaga in 1794, and died June 20, 1820 ae 56 years. A Revolutionary soldier and prominent in civil affairs and agriculture.

Deacon Archibald Fellows died Feb. 12, 1865 aged 70 year.

Barent Filkins died Jan. 17, 1863, aged 69 years. He was an assessor in 1828, and a man of note.

Joshua Forman was born in Dutchess county in 1777, came to Onondaga in 1800, died Aug. 4, 1849. Samuel Forman, his brother, died Sept. 7, 1852, aged 64 years. Owen Forman, a younger brother died in 1831. Their father, Joseph, was buried at Onondaga Valley.

Major Samuel S. Forman was born at Matteawan, NY July 6, 1767 and died Aug. 18, 1862. He was the youngest son of another Samuel, and was on the Mississippi in 1789 with a brother. While living in Cazenovia, he gave his name to Delphi. In 1808 he came to Salina and married Miss Sarah McCarty.

Robert Furman was an elder in the Park Presbyterian church at its organization in 1846, and was an alderman in 1848. He had been village trustee.

John Garrison, innkeeper, was overseer of highways in 1825.

James Geddes, of honorable record, died Aug. 19, 1838, aged 75 years, and rests in Oakwood.

Henry Gifford was born in Harwich, Mass., came to Syracuse in 1821 and married Phebe Dickinson in 1826. He died June 20, 1872 in his 71st year.

Daniel Gilbert was justice of the peace in 1825.

The Rev. Nathaniel T. Gilbert came in June 1823, and died of cholera July 19, 1832, aged 46 years.

Libbeus Gilbert died in the spring of 1827, leaving his wife, Eunice, executrix of his will and sole legatee. She died Nov. 15, 1838, aged 30 years, being quite young when married.

William Gilchrist, who died in 1880 aged 78 years and is buried in Jamesville, seems the son of William who died in 1803.

Pharis Gould, Jr. was born in Mass., Dec. 20, 1789 and came to Skaneateles in 1810, where he married Melissa Osborn. Later he went to Buffalo, but died in New York City Aug. 24, 1862. He was in the New York Assembly in 1838-40.

Amos P. Granger was born in Conn., came to Manlius in 1801, and from Onondaga Hill to Syracuse as a merchant. He married Charlotte Hickox, born 1790, died July 4, 1882. He was a village trustee in 1825, a Congressman later, a prominent member of St. Paul's church, and died Aug. 20, 1866, aged 77 years.

DeWitt C. Greenfield was born in Cayuga county, Nov. 22, 1818, was surrogate in 1865 and supervisor of Van Buren six times. He married Harriet Foster, March 1841, he died in Baldwinsville March 23, 1899.

John Greenway was born in England, Jan. 6, 1821 and came to Syracuse in 1837, where he became a noted brewer. He married Miss Nancy A. Hall, Feb. 18, 1848. His barbecue in Syracuse was a great event.

George Hall died May 20, 1840, aged 69 years. He came to Onondaga Valley in 1802 as a lawyer; was surrogate in 1811 and later was elected to Congress in 1818.

Jabez Hawley died Oct. 12, 1881, aged 69 years, and was on the vestry of St. Paul's church in 1826.

Thomas B. Heermans was Captain of the first fire company in 1825 and was buried in Rose Hill, June 29, 1863 aged 75 years.

Duncan Hillis came to Syracuse in 1837, was surrogate in 1844 and died Feb. 20, 1859.

Johnson Hall was born in Mass Jan. 6, 1794 and died Oct 27 1870. He came to Syracuse from LaFayette in 1838, and creditably filled many offices.

Jonathan P. Hicks died July 3, 1866 in his 76th year. In 1837 he was president of Liverpool village.

Frederick Horner's stone gives no date, but makes his age 78 years and 6 months.

Abel House died in 1836, age 40 years.

Parley Howlett, Sr., came from Vermont and died July 19, 1803 in his 49th years. He is buried at Howlett Hill, named from him.

Parley Howlett, Jr. was born in Shaftsbury, VT and died May 18, 1861 age 77 years. In 1805 he married Phebe Robbins.

Albion Jackson, son of Calvin, lived near the Indian Reservation in 1849, and had a son buried at Onondaga Valley in 1834, over nine years old.

Richard C. Johnson was an early merchant in Salina.

Col. Johnson, several times mentioned near the Cinder road, lived on the Kellogg Tract, and on his farm was held the great Camp Onondaga in 1853, a grand military gathering of several days duration. Gov. Seymour reviewed the troops.

Archy Kasson came from Auburn and was a vestryman of St. Paul's church in 1826. Ambrose Kasson was in the hook and ladder company of 1827 and also village justice.

James Keith died at Liverpool, May 31, 1885 in his 94th year.

Ashbel Kellogg's daughter married Thomas G. Alvord, and Mr. K., after presiding over the Bank of Salina, went to Michigan in 1845, dying there in 1848.

Cyrus Kinne, pioneer died at Fayettville, Aug. 1, 1808, aged 62 years.

William B. Kirk died Jan. 8, 1886, aged 87 years. He was village president in 1830 and his son was elected mayor, 1889.

William Lard came to Onondaga Hill, where he died by suicide in Oct. 1802.

Samuel Larned died Feb. 8, 1864 in his 73rd year. He was a village trustee in 1837, and otherwise prominent.

Benjamin Colvin Lathrop died Apr. 5, 1884, aged 86 years. John L. Lathrop died Sept. 15, 1856 age 66 years and was a trustee in 1837. His tavern was at the corner of Genesee and Walnut streets, on the south side of the former.

Grove Lawrence died Dec. 22, 1866, aged 71 years, being a lawyer of note, and long resident of Camillus.

Judge James Little was born in New Jersey, Mar. 25, 1799 and died Jan. 21, 1877. He married Elizabeth Smith and lived in the Village of Belgium,. For sixteen years he was supervisor of the Town of Clay.

Cornelius Longstreet died Dec. 17, 1814 aged 37 years. He married Deborah, daughter of Comfort Tyler, and they deeded an arsenal lot to the State, but the arsenal was built lower down the hill.

Elisha W. Leavenworth was born in Canaan, Columbia County, came to Syracuse in 1827, was mayor in 1849 and 1859, and died Nov. 24, 1887, aged 84 years.

Constant Luther died Nov. 21, 1830, aged 34 years.

James Lynch was in the U.S. Navy in 1812. He came here in 1825; was alderman in 1848, and died Apr. 7, 1876, aged 87 years and 5 months.

William Malcolm died Sept. 9, 1844 aged 62 years. He was village president in 1826.

John J. Mang, a German pioneer, and father of Mrs. Thomas Wheeler, died Dec. 16, 1842 aged 84 years.

James Mann, early merchant at Onondaga Hill, born in Woburn, Mass, Feb. 15, 1767, came to Onondaga in 1817 and to Syracuse in 1821. He died in Aurora, Cayuga County, Sept. 22, 1835, while visiting there. He was a vestryman of St. Pauls Church in 1826.

Jonas Mann died Sept. 22, 1835, aged 67 years. He was a village president.

Asa Marvin came from Oneida County and was father-in-law of John D. Norton, and partner of Elbert Norton who died in 1832.

Thomas McCarthy died June 30, 1848 aged 61 years. He was an early merchant and salt manufacturer. Dennis McCarthy was born March 19, 1814 and died Feb. 15, 1886. He was the son of Thomas and was a leading merchant and influential man.

Michael Mead died Nov. 5, 1849 aged 68 years.

Nicholas Mickles died Aug. 17, 1827 aged 57 years. He was one of the founders of the Presbyterian Church, Onondaga Valley in 1809. Philo D, Mickles, hardware merchant, died April 19, 1874 in his 76th year. He was village president in 1844.

Gad Miller, Revolutionary soldier and signer of the response in 1824, died Nov. 23, 1838 aged 72 years.

Allen Monroe died Nov. 10, 1884 and came to Syracuse in 1847, He was mayor in 1854 and in the New York Senate in 1860.

"Cabbagehead Moore" appears to be Ebenezer Moore, a pensioner from Mass., still living at the Valley in 1840, then 81 years old.

Dr. Gordon Needham came to Onondaga Valley in 1795 and taught school there the next year. He received his medical diploma when but seventeen and died in 1864, aged 84 years. He was a prominent Free Mason.

Henry Newton was village president in 1828.

John D. Norton died in 1861, a prominent man.

The Nukerck stone is now in Oakwood Cemetery, and reads, "Benjamin Nukerck died 7th Dec. 1787, aged 37 years." It was on farm lot 310, near south Geddes street, and in the rear of William Hudson's house on West Genesee street. He probably came from Ulster county. He was not murdered but died of delirium tremens, and Webster gave a graphic account of his burial. He tried to dig a grave but the drunken Indians tumbled into it faster than he could get them out. At last he was rid of them and finished his gloomy task undisturbed.

John W. O'Blennis died in 1813, aged 36 years and his wife, Catherine Van Vleck, died in 1871 aged 93 years.

Hezikiah Olcott of Pompey, died suddenly in 1800 and was buried with military honors.

Thomas Orman came from Pennsylvania and gave [the] name Orman's Landing in Harbor Brook, which probably had its name from such uses, Clark's account being untenable. In 1797 he commanded a military company in Lysander.

Joel Owen had a bowling alley and was in the first fire company.

Jared Parker was village trustee in 1845.

Sanford C. Parker of Baldwinsville, came there from Marcellus and held several public offices. He was born Feb. 4, 1800 and died April 26, 1861. In 1850 he was first master of Seneca River Lodge F. & A. M.

Asa Parks, Revolutionary soldier and living in 1824 was born in 1755 and became a pensioner in 1820.

In 1878 Arthur Patterson was the oldest surviving member of Onondaga Lodge F. & A.M., established at Onondaga Valley in 1803.

James Pease, according to others, "came from Lysander where he cut timer on his father's farm, hauled it to Baldwinsville, had it sawed and framed and soon after 1820 floated it on a scow, via the new waterway and the Seneca river to the lake, and thence to Syracuse and built his store." Many such small frames were made at Baldwinsville in early days, and two were recently standing there.

Andrew Pharis died May 16, 1843, aged 81 years. Simon Paris died in Geddes, his brother Andrew being administrator, May 14, 1817. His widow is buried in South Onondaga.

Deacon Ralph R. Phelps was an elder in Park Presbyterian church at its organization in 1846 and became a member of the first church in 1833. He was born in Preble July 18, 1809, married Elizabeth Ames 24 Oct. 1833 and died Nov. 15, 1873. He was not the Ralph R. Phelps of Manlius.

Samuel Phelps died in 1861, aged 61 years.

Elijah Phillips died May 14, 1845, aged 63 years. Amanda Danforth, his wife, was the first white child born in Onondaga county. She was born Oct. 14, 1789 and died Nov. 1, 1831 aged 42 years.

Morris Pratt died at Onondaga Valley, July 19, 1872, aged 71 years.

Hiram Putnam came here in 1829 and died Nov. 8, 1874 aged 84 years. He was village trustee in 1832 and an early vestryman in St. Paul's church.

Lewis H. Redfield died July 14, 1882 and was born in Conn. Nov. 26, 1793. He began the Onondaga Register in 1814; came to Syracuse from Onondaga Valley in 1829, and was a man of note. He married Anna Maria Treadwell in 1820, prominent in education work and highly esteemed. She died in 1889, aged 89 years.

Patrick Riley did his work and took care of the sick--day and night--in a fever epidemic in the salt fields.

John Rodgers came in 1823 and was a village trustee in 1825.

Thomas Rose was a salt inspector --1834-35.

Elijah Rust died July 13, 1824, aged 57 years, and is buried in Jamesville.

Shubael Safford, killed in building the Syracuse House, was the grandfather of John D. Safford.

John Savage died June 6, 1847, aged 64 years and Richard [Savage], April 11, 1885 aged 68 years.

Joseph Savage was superintendent of the Onondaga Coarse Salt company and village trustee in 1842.

Daniel O. Salmon died Feb. 9, 1902 in his 86th year. He was alderman in 1852 and 1853 and was long senior warden of St. James church.

Henry Seymour of Pompey, died in Utica, Aug. 26, 1837 aged 56 years. He was the father of Gov. Horatio Seymour, born at Pompey Hill in 1811.

Miles Seymour was trustee of the First Presbyterian church in 1824.

Henry Shattuck was born in Pompey Sept. 11, 1811 and came to Syracuse in 1826 as a real estate dealer. He married Mehitabel Knapp in 1821, and Sarah F. Park in 1842. He spent six years in Jamesville and died April 22, 1883.

Joseph Slocum, father of Mrs. Russell Sage, died March 30, 1863 in his 68th year. He was an assessor in 1844-45.

Stephen Smith came to Syracuse in 1821, and was agent of the Onondaga Salt company in 1831. He was born Oct. 25, 1776 and died March 23, 1854.

Deacon Thomas Spencer appears in the Baptist church records in 1821. He was a boat builder and salt manufacturer and died Mar. 5, 1872 aged 76 years. Eliza, his wife, died April 2, 1824 and was the first person buried in the "old cemetery" [at the] corner of West Water and Franklin streets.

David Stafford, born in 1803, was still living in 1885.

Amos Stanton, who came to Syracuse in 1805, died Aug. 14, 1806 aged 66 years. He was a short, stout man of light complexion. Rufus Stanton, his son, born in Mayfield, NY died Sept. 10, 1874 aged 86 years, and then said to be the oldest resident of the county. He married Minerva Belknap in 1815, and Minerva Phelps in 1824.

Baron Steuben has a stately monument over his grave in a secluded forest. He was born Nov. 15, 1830 and came to America in '77 and made the army efficient. He died Nov. 28, 1794, soon after his visit here.

George Stevens was born in Onondaga July 6, 1808 and died April 7, 1878. He was a president of the Village of Syracuse. In 1831 he married Harriet Stebbins and Mrs. Lydia P. Fitch in 1840.

Col. William Stevens, first salt superintendent, died Mar. 1, aged 51 years. He was an artillery captain in the Revolution and is buried in Elbridge where he was a pioneer.

Capt. William Stewart, who died Apr. 9, 1874 aged 69 years, was Mayor of Syracuse in 1865-67.

Col. William L. Stone, author of the "Life of [Joseph?] Brant, Etc" published his journals of these interesting trips. He was born Apr. 20, 1792 and died at Saratoga Aug 15 1844.

Oliver R. Strong died Oct. 3, 1872, aged 91 years. He came in 1802. Besides holding judicial offices, he was the first president of the Onondaga County Bank in 1830.

Oliver Teall, born in Conn. Aug. 5, 1788, died Aug. 15 1857. In 1809 he married Catherine Walter. He served in the War of 1812, and was superintendent of the canal at its opening. He was a man of broad views and varied business.

Dr. Salmon Thayer came from Onondaga to Geddes and died there.

Paschal Thurber died Dec. 26, 1874 aged 71 years. He was a village trustee in 1840 and was widely known.

John H. Tomlinson married Harriet, eldest daughter of James L. Voorhees. His father was a pioneer in Camillus.

Roswell Tousley was loan commissioner in 1811. Sylvenus Tousley died Mar. 30, 1838, aged 58 years. He was elected to the New York Assembly in 1836, and held judicial office.

Comfort Tyler died in Montezuma Aug. 5, 1827 aged 63 years. He was the first settler who made salt and was a man of note.

Harmon VanBuren died Apr. 24, 1887 aged 88 years. He filled many offices well.

Henry VanHeusen, in 1827, made the hooks for the first hook and ladder company.

Andrew N. VanPatten died Jan. 29, 1847 aged 65 years. In 1828 he managed a grand military ball, celebrating President Jackson's election.

Isaac Van Vleck died May 19, 1801, aged 58 years.

James L. Voorhees, "tall pine of Lysander", died Dec. 19, 1865 aged 71 years.

Peter Wales who died Nov. 22, 1824, aged 41, was the first butcher in Syracuse.

Elisha F. Wallace who died Aug. 15, 1870 aged 78 was a lawyer but became a salt manufacturer. He was the father of Judge William J. Wallace.

Herman Wallbridge was a trustee of the First Presbyterian church in 1824 and also a village trustee.

Judge James Webb was elected assessor in 1825 and was a village trustee. He built the fist stone house in Syracuse. He was six ft. high and fine looking. He died in Illinois.

Ephriam Webster died on the Tonawanda Reservation Oct, 1824 aged 62. He was of good reputation and fair education. The treatment of his Indian wife may well be discredited as well as some picturesque stories. He married Hannah Danks Nov. 19 1796 and was the first supervisor of the Town of Onondaga.

Thurlow Weed, who learned printing here and who died Nov. 22, 1882 aged 85, had pleasant notes on Onondaga in his reminiscences. He was long the able editor of the Albany Evening Journal.

Luke Wells was one of the first trustee of Danforth, in 1875, and an officer of the Congregational church there in 1884.

Dr. Amos Westcott died July 6, 1873 aged 59 years. He was the father of Edward N. and Rev. Frank N. Westcott, and was alderman in 1849 and mayor in 1860.

Charles A. Wheaton presided in the Board of Education in 1853. He afterwards went to Minnesota. Horace Wheaton died in 1882 aged 79. He was elected to Congress in 1842, and was Mayor in 1860. Both came from Pompey.

Thomas Wheeler died Mar. 30, 1862 aged 81 years.

Horatio N. White was the architect of the fine old court house and other notable buildings. He died in 1892.

Dr. John M. Wieting died Feb. 13, 1888 aged 76. He was born in Otsego county and came to Syracuse in 1837 where he soon became a man of note as a citizen and lecturer.

John Wilkinson died Sept. 19, 1862 aged 64 years. He was brought to Skaneateles in 1799 when an infant and was the first lawyer in Syracuse to which he gave its present name. He was prominent in railroad affairs. In 1825 he married Henrietta W. Swart.

Dr. Mather Williams was born Feb. 3, 1799 and died Dec. 10, 1868. He settled here in 1825. He married Judge Forman's second daughter. He had a drug store.

Othhniel H. Williston kept the old Mansion House in 1825.

Thaddeus M. Wood died Jan. 10, 1836 aged 64 years, He was born in Lenox, Mass. He came here in 1794 and married Miss Patty Danforth who died in 1854

Jason C. Woodruff died July 16, 1878 aged 78 year. He married Amanda Johnson in 1826. He joined the First Presbyterian Church in May 1852 and was thrice president of the Onondaga County Agricultural Society and in 1852 he was Mayor. He was of middle height but very strong.

Henry Young died Nov. 11, 1851 aged 60 years and was a village trustee in 1826. John Young died at Orville Sept. 9, 1834, aged 82 years. He was a signer of the Veterans Response in 1824.

I think it well to add to the above some scattered notes by various persons, of the days of which Mr. Cheney told so much. The county and town centennial celebrations in 1794 [1894?] brought out much of interest, and the whole proceedings in all these cases might well be published by the Historical Association, as was intended. At present they only exist in papers published 20 years ago. Of most of these, I preserved copies, as some others did, but full files should give much more. Two of the town celebrations had but slight connection with Syracuse but the one at Onondaga Valley was more in touch with the city.

Miles T. Frisbee read a creditable poem on "Onondaga's Centennial" and out of the 154 lines of this a few may be quoted:

"Now Ephriam Webster, sturdy pioneer,
A man of iron heart, devoid of fear,
Up Onondaga's stream, on either hand
Explores the borders of his promised land.
Making the savages his firm allies;
Unfaltering when taken by surprise,
though dangers dire and many perils passed,
Escapes them all and dies in peace at last.
Here Asa Danforth comes to pitch his tent -
The first real founder of the settlement.
Like Webster, a New Englander by birth,'
The hardiest stock of pioneers on earth!
With him is Comfort Tyler, chain in hand
and trusty compass to survey the land;
Then Longstreet, Forman, Needham, Sabine, Hall,
Swan, Geddes, Hopper, Mickles, Wood, and all
the pioneers came on without delay,
As their descendants gather here to-day."

John T. Roberts, our best authority on pioneer days in Onondaga Valley, that year gave some notes on pioneer homes there, though there have been some changes since. As the list is valuable and brief it is here given in full and in Mr. Roberts own words:

The Pratt house on the Tully turnpike, west side, is probably the oldest house in the Valley. Opposite to it is the site of Gen. Thad. M. Wood's residence.

The Ephriam Webster house (1796) is on the Bostwick farm, west of the valley.

John Forman's house (1798), west end of village, on Seneca turnpike, known as the "red house" is occupied by Sidney Wood, colored, formerly a slave of Thad. M. Wood.

John Hastings house (1800) is north of the village, west side.

William Sabine's house (1808) is back of the academy and occupied by his widow and T. W. Meachem.

Joshua Forman's house (1808), on the Seneca turnpike, north side, is occupied by Dr. Whitford.

Jasper Hoppers' house (1800) is occupied by Mr. Loomis.

Samuel Forman's house (1812), south side of turnpike is occupied by Mark Potter.

Phil Gridley's stone house (1812), east end of village, on turnpike, is owned by R. R. Slocum.

John VanPelt's brick house (1812) later known as Pattersons', west side of village, Main street, is owned by E. J. Kline.

John Adams old stage house (1802), foot of west hill, is occupied by W. H. Harrison.

Arthur Patterson's house and store (1820) are occupied by W. H. Card.

Rev. Dr. Caleb Alexander's house (1820) south of the village, is owned by the estate of Lemuel Clark.

The Town Hall and Odd Fellows Hall (1808).

The Mercer Mill (1813) was built by Joshua Forman and others.

The Fuller house, corner of Midland and Main street, was constructed from several old stores and dwellings.

Dr. Tolman's barn has a frame made from the timbers of the old Danforth house.

The John Adams house, one of the oldest dwellings, is the Dorwin residence at the springs.

Most early explorers mention the salt works. When Elkanah Watson was here in 1791, he said: "With some difficulty we found the creek on which the salt works are now erected, half a mile from the mouth at the foot of the hill. These works are in a rude, unfinished state but are capable of making about 8,000 bushels per anum, which is nearly the quantity required for the present consumption of the country." The next year another writer reported, "That sixteen bushels of salt are daily manufactured at Major's Danforths works at the Salt Springs," and that Mr. "Van Vleck, formerly of Kinderhook, is erecting other works at the same place."

Mrs. Margaret Treadwell Redfield Smith, daughter of Lewis H. Redfield, furnished many interesting notes from her father's papers. His list of early settlers is valuable. He brought the first iron printing press used here, and also introduced the composition roller in place of the ink balls which had been in use over 300 years. In my father's office I have used both.

I quote one historical incident from Mrs. Smith notes: "General Lafayette passed through the Hollow on his way from Onondaga Hill to Syracuse, on the occasion of his visit in 1826. The magnates of the county were present - a very remarkable company gathered - old pioneers, Revolutionary soldiers, and of the War of 1812, walking in picturesque twos and threes in procession, under the bowery of evergreen arches, erected in his honor over the broad, main street of the Hollow. A multitude greeted him at Syracuse, where a dinner was given in his honor, at the hotel on the site of the present Empire House. The Hollow had its special tradition of the occasion. As the procession passed along the street it was arrested and stopped when it came in front of Mr. Redfield's house, and Mrs. Redfield presented a bouquet of flowers which the General gracefully accepted.

"Lafayette's speech, in answer to the address of welcome on the occasion of his visit, as reported in the *Onondaga Register*, was as follows:

"The names of Onondaga and Syracuse, on behalf of whose population you are pleased so kindly to welcome me, recall to my mind at the same time the wilderness that, since the time I commanded on the northern frontier, has been transformed into one of the most populous, well cultivated and enlightened parts of the United States, and the ancient Sicilian city, once the seat of republican institutions, much inferior however, to those which in American Syracuse are founded upon the plain investigation, the unalloyed establishment of the rights of men, and upon the best representative forms of government. No doubt, sir, that among co-operators of the Revolution the most sanguine of us could not fully anticipate the rapidity of the improvements which, on a journey of many thousand miles (the tour alone, from Washington to this place, amounts to five thousand miles), have delighted me, and of which this part of the country offers a bright example. Be pleased to accept my personal thanks, and in behalf of the people of Onondaga and Syracuse, to receive the tribute of my sincere and grateful acknowledgement.' "An engraved likeness of Lafayette was circulated, which bore the following inscription: 'The Nation's Guest. Commemoration of the Magnanimous and Illustrious, Lafayette's Visit to the United States of North America, in the Forty-fourth year of her Independence.' White satin badges, with likeness and text are rarely seen as fine as that issued of Lafayette at this time."

Mention has been made of Thurlow Weed famous in anti-Masonic times, for, "A good enough Morgan 'till after election" and equally famous organization leader. It is fair to say that he explained the above words. When Thomas C. Fay established the Lynx at Onondaga Valley, he took young Weed as an apprentice. Before that he used to help his father in getting out cord wood for the salt boilers. Then he found winter work at Mickles' furnace, and summer work on farms. He had one adventure of which any boy would be proud to-day, which he thus described:

"In the spring of 1810, with two other boys, I was walking of a pleasant evening in the vicinity of Onondaga Creek, a mile and a half south of the site of the present City of Syracuse, then a tangled swamp inhabited mainly by frogs, water snakes and owls, Upon the creek stood Wood's mill. below which for several rods were rifts. Out attention and surprise were excited by seeing bright lights moving, as we supposed, along the banks of the creek. On approaching however, we discovered Onondaga Indians with pine-knot torches and clubs, killing salmon, whose fins and backs were seen as they were ascending the creek in shallow water over the rifts. The Indians good naturedly lent us clubs and gave us the benefit of their torches, until each had captured a salmon, with which we departed for our homes in jubilant spirits. Most of the inhabitants of Syracuse will find it hard to believe that salmon ever taken south of that city. And yet such is a fact, for which my friend Philo D. Mickles, recently deceased, would have vouched, as he was one of my companions on the occasion."

It will be noticed that John Durnford sold lottery tickets in his bookstore, lotteries being in good repute then.

The New York Literature Fund was substantially helped in 1801 by four lotteries, authorized by the Legislature. Lotteries were authorized for Union College, Schenectady, in 1805, 1814, and 1822, and it may have been the latter in which Mr. Durnford was interested. The learned professions all aided these, and several men sold lottery tickets here.

The third county court house had long been a striking feature of Syracuse. On Onondaga Hill, Thomas T. Davis long ago said: "The first court house was graced by the presence of such jurists as Kent, Van Ness, and Livingstone, and witnessed the forensic triumphs of such advocates as James Emott, Thomas Addis Emmett, Martin VanBuren, Egbert Benson and Abraham VanVechten." A goodly array of names mostly forgotten. At one time several lawyers lived there.

In 1894 Mrs,. Charlotte (Malcolm) Dillaye indulged in some childish recollections, a few of which follow:

"My father, William Malcolm, was one of the first settlers and pioneers of Onondaga county. When he commenced business in a country store in the little hamlet of Syracuse, it contained four buildings, viz: one house and tavern, one store and one blacksmith shop. My father built the second house where I was born, and which connected with Salt Point by an Indian path through the woods. The Malcolm Block stands on the site. The store was opposite the canal. The Weiting block stands on the spot.

"A packet boat, containing passengers, went through twice a week, and afterwards daily, stopping for a few moments at the canal basin, opposite my father's store. This was a great event, and when the dock bell rang out announcing the arrival , the news spread that the packet boat had come. The other means of conveyance was the stage coach. In this way my father went to New York, for goods, twice every year.

"My father was chosen treasurer for the Onondaga tribe of Indians, and on pay day it was almost impossible to get inside the store for the crowd of Indians and squaws who brought their government money for him to take care of. At these times the numerous papooses, strapped on frames, leaned up against the store front, much as bulletin boards do now."

Mrs. Caroline Hargin, ninth child of Gen. John Ellis, gave some account of her father. She was born in 1812, and died in 1820. When Lafayette passed through, the widow harnessed the horses to the big wagon, loaded up nine children, and got an early start to see the hero. It was the next day, however, that they saw him. "I remember perfectly well how he looked. He was dressed so elegantly and so fashionably. I could not get very near him, because there was such a crowd about him, but I saw him distinctly."

Mrs. Hargin's recollections of the old slavery times here are noteworthy. "Her father found it so difficult to get farm hands that he took a trip to Virginia and purchased four slaves - Sam, Chris, Peter and Chloe. They were all with the family when Mrs. Hargin was born and were afterwards liberated by Mrs. Ellis. Slaves were kept by Jasper Hopper, by Judge Curtis, and by a number of other prominent settlers."

The Rev. Samuel Brace (1870) said: "Pompey had its slaves; a number were held on the Hill by some of the most respectable families, but treated not as slaves in the South were said to be, but with much lenity and kindness. They were however, numerous in the northwestern part of town, near what is now Jamesville: sundry families there, as the DeWitts and Depuys, held numbers of then and with their labor entered largely into the cultivation of tobacco." In the will of Jacobus DePuy, Surrogates office, is this clause: He gives to his wife "the black girl, Bet, said black girl to be free at the decease of my said beloved wife."

Another pioneer in 1894 said: "There were slaves here then. You didn't know that? Yes, bless you, lots of them. There was old Thad Wood, the lawyer; he had a slave maid in his family. Squire Sabine had a man slave. Lots of the old settlers had them. They used them well, too, and sent them to school. Why there was old Squire Sabine's slave, he used to carry a watch and dress like a lord. Judge Forman had a slave, and when he went away he made provision for her support."

The same old settlers said: "Comfort Tyler, when I first saw him was a white-headed old man and I was only 17 or 18. Harvey Baldwin? Why I remember his father - Jonas C. Baldwin. They lived in what was called the gulf, up near where Brighton is now. Harvey came here and studied law and my father worked for him for years. He was a very smooth - polished, well-greased man, so to speak, as his father was also.

St. Paul's Church, Syracuse was originally a mission of Zion Church, Onondaga Hill, but had its present organization in 1826. John Durnford and Samuel Wright were the wardens; Amos P. Granger, Archy Kasson, Mather Williams, James Mann, Matthew W. Davis, Barent Filkins, Othniel Q. Williston and Jabez Hawley, vestrymen. Bishop Hobart visited that year.

Mr. J. Backus Ives, one of B. Davis Noxon's twelve children also remembered Lafayette at Onondaga Hill:

"He came over the old state road from Marcellus in a buggy. He had just been entertained there. Everybody on the Hill rushed down to the hotel to see and shake hands with him. He came early in the morning and when he reached the hotel there went into the dining-room, with a crowd following him and had breakfast. When he came out he shook hands with everyone except myself. I was too bashful. As I remember Lafayette he was rather stout and very good looking. I remember seeing him bow to the people as he rode past.

"We moved to this city in 1829 and lived in the house on James street next to the Keble school. There were no houses on Foot street as it was then called with the exception of one on the other side quite a way up. The Leavenworth house had not been thought of. Prospect Hill was all forest and Foot's settlement, to the east of James street hill was approached by way of Foot street. At the site of the priest's home at the corner of Lock and West Willow streets, lived Elder Gilbert, a Baptist minister who died of cholera in 1832. The house we lived in was owned by the Townsend & James Company of Albany. A year later my father bought a lot from this company at the corner of Church (now West Willow) and North Salina streets. Straight across the street afterwards stood the old County Clerk's office, and on another corner was the Onondaga House. My father, who afterward became Judge Noxon, put up a handsome brick house, which now stands. This was on Church street, just west of the corner where Mr. Stoecker has his jewelry store. This block was built a short time afterwards by my father and since sold by him. My father had a law office in the block next to our house. Among the clerks in the office, Elias W. Leavenworth was studying law. A short time afterwards George F. Comstock, then a young law student, came up from Utica and studied law in my father's office. There were two other houses in the block, one owned by Gen. Amos P. Granger, and the other by Hiram Deming, a clerk of Mr. Granger's, and who married Mr. Granger's niece. The three houses were considered at that time the finest in the city and Church street was the most fashionable."

Hon. Thomas G. Alvord's reminiscences are of interest. He was born at Onondaga Valley, but his father returned to Lansingburgh, NY making a visit to Salt Point in 1816 with his six-year old boy. The drive occupied from Monday morning to Saturday night. Besides the Bogardus tavern there were two shanties and one house in Syracuse. Salina had from 250 to 300 inhabitants. After several visits he settled in the latter village in 1833. His account of the salt industry follows:

"In the early part of the century the blocks were all situated in the marsh near the bluff. The water was raised by an ordinary pump, worked by hand. Huge trees, hollowed like canoes, were the cisterns, and the water was carried to the kettles in pails. The largest block contained eight kettles, four on a side. Most of the salt was made in the winter, the wood for boiling being cut in the neighborhood. The product was stored in warehouses and in the spring was barreled for shipment to distant points. The supply of the territory for 100 miles distant was secured in the winter when the sleighing was good.

In the spring, the supply for the west was shipped to Oswego in bateaux, carrying from 10 to 25 barrels, The Southwestern and Pennsylvania trade was transported in the same way, by way of Cortland, and following the water courses to the Chenango and Chemung rivers, where the barrels were loaded on rafts of timber for points on the Ohio and other rivers. To get to New York the cargo was started on a small boat on Onondaga lake, the outlet of the Seneca river, thence to Three River Point, where the Oneida river and lake were used to Wood Creek. Then the route was to the Mohawk and to Schenectady and Albany, where sloops took the cargo to New York. All supplies from New York were brought by this route, and it required from four to six months to make the round trip, with salt one way and merchandise the other.

"The winters were enlivened by the farmers who came to barter their produce for salt, and the Indians who chopped wood while the snow was on the ground. I have seen the tavern all filled, and the houses of the residents with all they could accommodate of farmers, who came as far as 100 miles for loads of salt. I have seen the Indians in their war paint and trappings, just as they appeared in the War of 1812 - all mounted on spirited horses and executing their wild manoeuvers.

"My father and my uncle engaged in mercantile business and built in 1808 the first brick building west of Schenectady, at what is now the corner of North Salina and Exchange streets. The building is standing yet. The brick was made on the banks of Yellow creek, which ran a little north of the Mowry, and the stone was quarried. The structure was used as a hotel and later as a business house."

Among the floats in the Centennial celebration were representations of the old blockhouse, the Mansion House, the first canal boat, Comfort Tyler's salt boiling, and other scenes of early life. In 1895 the Historical Association voted to publish the full records of this great event, but it was not done and only newspaper account survive. Soon after that Mrs. W. W. Teall gathered up many pathetic tales and records of the women of Onondaga, which are to appear in the next volume.

Blair, William K. 12, 82
Blake, Harry 22
Bogardus, --- (Mr.) 4, 22
  Henry 15, 16, 52, 82
  Peter 15, 82
Bogardus Corners 6
Bogardus Tavern 102
Bonta, J. O. 80
Booth, --- 13
  Samuel 11, 16, 48, 69
Bostwick, --- 95
  William 66
Brace, --- 83
  Elizur 83
  Samuel 100
Brant, Joseph 92
Brighton 101
Briscoe, William 81
Brockway, --- 20
Brown, --- (Gen.) 9
  D. 28
  John C. 3, 82
Brownson, Orestes A. 12
Buel, --- (Mr.) 40
Buffalo Creek Reservation
  79
Bulkley, William 52
Burdick, George W. 27, 30
Burgess, Jacob 52
Burnet, --- (Maj.) 20
  Helen (Creed) 82
  M. D. (Mrs.) 12
  Moses D. 45, 82
Burnet Park 82
Burnett, --- (Maj.) 45
  M. D. 29
  Moses D. 53
Burns, John 28
Burton, Burr 82
Butler, --- 62
  Ebenezer 82

Butler, Townsend & Co. 41
Butts, Horace 67, 82
  Mason 67, 82

Cadwell, S. W. 27
  Stephen 17, 83
  Stephen W. 20
Calley, James 52
Camillus 30
Canfield, D. 11, 13
Card, W. H. 96
Carey, --- (Mr.) 73
  Bradley 72, 73, 83
  Matilda (Phelps) 83
Carpenter, Benjamin 62
Carter, Charles 80
Case, Henry 52, 83
  Ruel 52
Centre House 22
Chamberlain, --- (Deacon) 44
  H. 83
Chapman, --- (Mr.) 71, 73
  Abner 39, 83
  Eliza (Merrick) 83
  Mary (Everingham) 83
Chase, Beverly 81
Cheney, --- 32, 45
  --- (Mr.) 6, 70, 73, 74, 78, 79,
    81
  Anne P. 2
  Frances M. 2
  George Nelson 1
  H. Nelson 1
  Horatio N. 27, 30
  Jerome L. 1
  L. A. 12, 69
  Loren L. 1, 27, 30
  Lucius 1
  Lucius H. 83
  Nelson 1
  Prentice Dana 2

106

Cheney, T. C. 70, 71, 72, 73
Timothy 1, 2
Timothy C. 73
Timothy Collingwood 1
Church's Grocer 22
Chusing, --- (Widow) 21
Circus House 23
Clapp, --- (Mr.) 48
Clark, --- (Mr.) 36, 37
Augusta M. (Peck) 83
E. L. 20
Elizur 72, 73, 74, 83
Ephraim 52
J. V. H. 81
Jerusha (Spencer) 83
Lemuel 96
Clarke, P. 12
Climax House 46
Clinton, --- (Gov.) 68, 80
Clinton Ditch 38
Clinton Square 16
Close, William B. 27, 30
Cobb, --- (Mr.) 48
Coburn & Hurst 74
Cody, Joel 13, 23
Coffin Block 32
Cohen, --- 13
Coklin, William 30
Collins, Luke 28, 83
Colton, --- (Dr.) 64
Walter 83
Colvin, --- (Dr.) 21, 22
B. F. 21
Benjamin 83
D. S. 29
David S. 83
Colwell & Thurber 80
Comstock, George F. 10, 83, 102
Conklin, John 28
William 27

Cook, --- (Mr.) 11
Ann Belden 2
C. 80
Harriet B. (Ellis) 83
Silas 2
William A. 83
William S. 29
Cook's Coffee House 35, 40
Cooper, --- (Mr.) 70
Corbin, Lewis 28
Corinth 6
Cossitt, R. O. 80
Sterling 10, 13, 16, 21, 83
Cossitt's Corners 83
Crawe, J. 28
Creed, --- (Widow) 12
Helen 82
John B. 52
John P. 83
Crofoot, LeGrand 44
William 44
Crouse, John 13
Cummings, --- 20
Cummins, --- (Col.) 54
Curtis, --- (Judge) 100
Elijah W. 29, 83
Fisher 52, 84
Medad 64, 65, 84
Oris 84
Curtiss, Medad 66
Cushing, --- (Chief Justice) 56

Dana, Daniel 13, 29, 84
J. D. 18
Danforth, --- 96
--- (Gen.) 61, 65
--- (Major) 96
Adams 84
Amanda 90
Asa 4, 58, 61, 62, 65, 84, 95

Danforth, Hannah (Wheeler)
84
John 58, 62, 84, 85
Olive (Langdon) 84
Patty 94
Rufus 52, 85
Daniels, --- (Dr.) 84
Danks, Catharine 9
Hannah 93
Darling, Benjamin 15, 85
Davis, Matthew L. 12, 16, 85
Matthew W. 85, 101
Thomas T. 29, 85, 99
Day, --- (Dr.) 51
Jonathan 85
Deming, Hiram 18, 102
Hiram A. 85
Denfee, Patrick 28
Denslow, --- (Mr.) 18
Depuy, --- 100
DePuy, Jacobus 100
DeWitt 30
DeWitt, --- 100
Moses 61, 85
Dexter, --- (Mr.) 58
Dickinson, Phebe 86
Pliny 29, 85
Dillaye, Charlotte (Malcolm)
99
Henry A. 85
Rene D. 85
Dillaye Black 42
Doran, --- 20
Doris, G. 81
Dorwin, --- 96
Drew, Oliver 28
Driscoll, --- (Mr.) 12
Dunford, --- (Mr.) 15
Dunn, John 15
Durant, W. 27
Durkee, William G. 28

Durnford, --- (Mr.) 13, 35
H. W. 14
Harry 40
Henry W. 34, 53, 64, 85
John 27, 30, 33, 39, 45, 53,
64, 85, 99, 101
Durston, John 21, 85
Dwight, Zebina 26, 30
Dwinelle, --- 40

Eagle Tavern 16
Earll, David 85
Jonas 85
Nehemiah H. 64, 85
Early, Daniel 64
Jonas 64
Eastman, --- (Mr.) 64
Eckford, --- (Mr.) 41
Henry 74
Elbridge 41
Eliker, John 28
Elizabethtown Point 55
Elliott, Daniel 16, 29, 86
Ellis, Caroline 100
Harriet B. 83
John 65, 86
Submit (Olds) 86
Elliston, --- (Miss) 28
Emerick, --- (Mr.) 73
Emmett, Thomas Addis 99
Emott, James 99
Empire Block 17
Everingham, Mary 83

Fay, Jonathan 52
Thomas C. 98
Featherly, Draper & Cole 74
Federal Company 62
Fellows, --- (Deacon) 11
Aaron 82
Archibald 86

111

Needham, --- 95
--- (Dr.) 4
Gordon 89
Newkirk, --- 10
Benjamin 8
Newton, Henry 13, 35, 89
Norton, C. T. 80
Elbert 89
John D. 17, 89
Noxon, --- (Judge) 102
B. Davis 101
Noxon Block 22
Nukerck 79
Nukerck, Benjamin 89

O'Blennis, --- (Mrs.) 61
Catherine (VanVleck) 90
John (Mrs.) 58
John W. 90
Ogle Tavern 22
Olcott, --- (Mr.) 61
Hezikiah 90
Josiah 58
Old Federal Springs 74
Old Sandy 48
Olds, Submit 86
Olmstead, --- 80
Onondaga East Hill 3, 4
Onondaga Hill 65, 99
Onondaga Hollow 4, 19, 34
Onondaga House 102
Onondaga Lake 63
Onondaga Salt Co. 74, 75
Orman, Thomas 61, 90
Orman's Landing 90
Ormsbee, L. J. 80
Osborn, Melissa 86
Osborn & Hunt 80
Ostrander, Thomas H. 28
Oundiaga 79
Owen, Celeste 82

Owen, Joel 90

Packwood, S. 28
Palby, Elby 52
Palladium, Morris 2
Palmer, --- (Mr.) 70
A. W. 2
A. W. (Mrs.) 3
Frances M. (Cheney) 2
William L. 12
Paris, Andrew 90
Simon 90
Park, Asa 15
Sarah F. 91
Parker, --- (Dr.) 25
George B. 18
J. H. 31
Jared 90
Jared H. 29
Sanford C. 70, 90
Parkhurst, Laura M. 82
Parks, Asa 90
Parsons, --- (Capt.) 15
Rufus 8, 10
Patten, --- (Mr.) 70, 71
Patterson, --- 10, 96
Arthur 4, 90
Pease, James 48, 49, 90
Peat, James 59
Peck, Augusta M. 83
Peck & Rudd 35, 80
Perkins, Erastus 52
Pfohl, --- (Mr.) 73
Pharis, Andrew 90
Simon 61
Phelps, --- (Dr.) 35
Elizabeth (Ames) 90
John B. 28
Matilda 83
Minerva 92
Ralph R. 90

115

* * NEW YORK * *

American Vital Records from the Baptist Register, 1824-1832 and the New York Baptist Register, 1832-1834, by Elizabeth Hayward. Includes a geographical locator guide. Abstracts of deaths & marriages from newspapers published in Utica, NY, but area of interest embraces eastern US. 105 pp., index, soft cover, $12.50.

ERIE COUNTY

Erie County, New York Obituaries As Found In The Files Of The Buffalo & Erie County Historical Society, 1812-1880. Obituaries abstracted from the holdings of the Buffalo & Erie County Historical Society arranged in alphabetical order by name of deceased. Each entry gives residence of deceased, place and date of death and age; most name family relations; some give cause of death. Many persons who moved west but originally resided in Erie County had their obituaries in the local newspapers and are named here. Introduction by Mary F. Bell, Director of Library & Archives, Erie Co. 8 1/2 x 11", soft bound, 340 pp., map, full-name index, 1992. $30.00

MADISON COUNTY

Deaths, Births, and Marriages From Newspapers Published in Hamilton, Madison Co., NY, 1818-1885. Records copied from newspapers in the Archives of Colgate Univ., Hamilton, Madison Co., NY. As vital records were not recorded in NY until after 1900, these abstracts help fill that void. 329 pp., index, soft cover. $28.00.

Abstracts from Madison Co., NY Newspapers in the Cazenovia, NY Library. Mary K. Meyer, Editor. Includes abstracts of marriages, deaths, etc. from the *Cazenovia Pilot*, beginning in 1808 and includes those of several other newspapers published in the village to c. 1850. Also includes abstracts from the *DeRuyter Gleaner* of the 1880's. Encompasses the area of Madison, Chenango, Oneida and Onondaga counties with scattered notices from other NY counties. Includes map of Madison Co., Geographical Locator Guide, 336 pp., indexed, soft cover. $30.00

ONONDAGA COUNTY

Early Marriages in Central New York Abstracted from Early Newspapers by William M. Beauchamp. (With An Appendix of Early Marriages and Deaths from Manlius, New York Newspapers by Harry C. Durston.) Information taken from various newspapers, predominantly those in Syracuse, Skaneateles, and Manlius covering a five-county area of Onondaga, Madison, Oswego, Cayuga and Cortland, and more scattered locations. Often indicates residence of former inhabitants of the area. Includes map of Onondaga Co. and Geographical Locator Guide. Alpha. order, index of secondary names. $17.00